303 Kid-Approved Exercises and Active Games

SmartFun Activity Books from Hunter House

303

Kid-Approved Exercises and Active Games

AGES 6–8

Kimberly Wechsler

Foreword by Darren S. McLaughlin
Illustrated by Michael Sleva

A Hunter House SmartFun Book

DEDICATION

I would like to dedicate this book to the thousands of children
who taught me how to bring together fitness and fun
and to the children and families who will benefit
from their teachings.

Hunter House Inc., Publishers
PO Box 2914
Alameda CA 94501-0914

Library of Congress Cataloging-in-Publication Data
Wechsler, Kimberly.
303 kid-approved exercises and active games : ages 6-8 / Kimberly Wechsler.
p. cm. — (Smart fun activity books)
Includes index.
ISBN 978-0-89793-619-4 (pbk.) — ISBN 978-0-89793-624-8 (spiral)
ISBN 978-0-89793-632-3 (ebook)
1. Exercise for children. 2. Physical fitness for children. I. Title.
GV443.W37 2012
613.7′042—dc23   2012030305

Project Credits

Cover Design: Jinni Fontana	Rights Coordinator: Candace Groskreutz
Book Production: John McKercher	Publisher's Assistant: Bronwyn Emery
Illustrator: Michael Sleva	Administrative Assistant: Kimberly Kim
Developmental and Copy Editor: Amy Bauman	Customer Service Manager: Christina Sverdrup
Managing Editor: Alexandra Mummery	Order Fulfillment: Washul Lakdhon
Editorial Assistant: Tu-Anh Dang-Tran	Administrator: Theresa Nelson
Special Sales Manager: Judy Hardin	Computer Support: Peter Eichelberger
Publicity Coordinator: Martha Scarpati	Publisher: Kiran S. Rana

Printed and bound by Bang Printing, Brainerd, Minnesota
Manufactured in the United States of America

9 8 7 6 5 4 3 2 1   First Edition   13 14 15 16 17

Contents

Introduction: Active Kids

The Exercises and Games

A list of the games indicating appropriate group sizes begins on the next page.

Please note that the illustrations in this book are all outline drawings. The fact that the pages are white does not imply that the people all have white skin. This book is for people of all races and ethnic identities.

List of Games

	Whole group	Any size group	Small groups	Pairs
	whole group	any size	small groups	pairs

Fitness Games

Balance

Most of the activities may be performed with groups of any size. A few are designed for pairs, small groups, or the whole group. These exceptions are individually marked with a group-size icon.

Foreword

2:38 PM. This was the time at which the bell would ring out my freedom every school day afternoon of my childhood. It was the mid-sixties, and I was one of the hordes of baby boomers who clamored out of the classroom, down the stairs, and into the schoolyard. The school day was over; the afternoon was mine. I headed straight for my bike—one of the literally hundreds of bikes waiting in the racks outside my elementary school. My friends from the neighborhood and I would pedal the mile from school to home as fast as we could to allow for as much playtime as possible before dinner. Once at home, we would change out of our "school clothes" and into our "play clothes," grab a quick snack, and hurry back outside to meet up with the rest of the kids.

A large field abutted the properties on our street, adjacent to a long row of greenhouses. Though nothing was ever grown in the field, it was frequently plowed to keep it from becoming overrun with weeds. We'd play Army, have dirt-bomb fights, build baseball fields, and run between the greenhouses. Woods at the end of the road separated our town from the next, and paths ran through the woods. Where one didn't exist, we'd clear one. We'd ride our bikes through the woods, climb trees, build forts and tree houses and, if we were lucky, maybe even talk our dads into sleeping out there overnight with us. In nicer weather, if we were feeling adventurous, we'd ride our bikes the two miles down to the bay and go fishing or clamming or just throw rocks as far as we could out into the water. On weekends and summer nights, all the kids in the neighborhood would get together for huge games of Flashlight Tag, Spud, and Red Light/Green Light. We were what a local elementary-school physical education teacher and good friend of mine likes to refer to as "range kids." Once the school bell set us free from the classroom, we were free to roam the town until the six o'clock whistle summoned us home to the dinner table.

That was quite some time ago, and life was different then. I know that many kids are still physically active today, but somehow it's not the same. Today we schedule our kids' activities. We pile them in minivans and SUVs and ferry them from dance class to soccer practice to swim meets as our blood pressure rises with the stress. We tell them to "go out there and have some fun and burn off some of that energy," but they don't seem to have the freedom for creative play that we did when we were younger. Their physical education programs at school have been cut to bare bones. Their lunch and recess breaks barely allow them the time to eat, let alone digest their food or perhaps run around a bit and get some fresh air before returning to the classroom. They have way too many hours of "screen time"—time spent staring at television screens, video games, cell phones, laptops, iPods, and iPads. Fast food is no longer the rare treat it was when it was still a relatively new option for dining out. For many of today's youth, it has become a staple meal in the hectic life of the "soccer mom." It's no wonder the nation is in the midst of an obesity epidemic.

Over the last thirty years, the rate of childhood obesity has tripled among youngsters ages six to eleven and doubled among those ages two to five and twelve to nineteen. Childhood obesity involves much more than simply being overweight; obesity in children can lead to a number of related health issues. Liver disease, heart disease, cancers, vascular disease, orthopedic issues, and diabetes have all presented in children who are obese. New evidence also suggests that this younger generation may be the first in history to have a shorter life expectancy than their parents.

Kim Wechsler saw this epidemic coming long before it hit the media by storm. I had the opportunity to work with Kim in the early 1990s and learned from her the importance of getting kids up and moving and active from an early age. I learned how the key to success with promoting this activity was to package it with just the right amount of education combined with a heaping helping of fun. I watched while Kim demonstrated with a spray bottle how the germs of an uncontrolled sneeze spread through the air; the kids laughed and learned how important it was to sneeze into your arm instead of freely into the air or into a hand that allows the germs to spread very easily. She created fun cardio programs that got kids up and running around without ever realizing how hard they were working. She stressed the importance of cooling down and stretching and relaxing after activity.

Kim taught me a lesson or two as well. She taught me what we can do to help our children. She encouraged us to avoid pre-prepared foods, which are high in preservatives, sugars, and fats; to limit the amount of snack and junk foods kept in our homes; and to provide foods for our children that are rich in fiber and have less than 30 percent of their calories derived from fat. She reminded us not to use foods as rewards or negotiating tools with our children. She also advised us to limit the amount of daily "screen time" our kids are exposed to. Most important of all, she taught us to plan family exercise. Go for a swim, a hike, or a walk together or even just throw the ball around the yard for a while—to make family exercise a special time for the family. Kim taught us that together we can make a difference in the health and well-being of our children and, most important, she taught us that it can actually be a lot of fun.

Darren S. McLaughlin, General Manager
Wayside Racquet & Swim Club, www.wayside.net

Acknowledgments

I would like to thank my children, Andrew and Addison, for twenty years of being my "advisory board" on all fitness games. You can retire now; I promise I won't call you and ask you for your opinions on fitness games—at least not tonight.

I would like to thank my friend and husband, Jonathan, for his loving support, his encouragement to follow my passion, his patience with my endless discussions about family fitness, and his many months of tireless proofreading.

To Mattie Rose and James McShan, Henry Ward Beecher once said that "Children are the hands by which we take hold of heaven."

And to the staff of Hunter House for their dedication to and support of healthy families.

My website is www.FitAmericanFamilies.com.

Introduction
Active Kids

Message to Parents, Teachers, and Counselors

I have built a career on teaching fitness to children, teens, and adults. Designing exercises for families must be a thoughtful process; no program should be "one size fits all." Some movements that work well for one particular age group could prove disastrous for another age group. Each age group is uniquely different physiologically and intellectually, and each group is motivated by different factors. My mission as a family fitness specialist is to design exercise programs that provide and incorporate the latest research on health and fitness trends, take into consideration the best practices for each family member, and then offer a deep understanding and a big-picture perspective of keeping families fit. This book has been written specifically for children six to eight years old. The exercises in this book are age and skill appropriate for most children in this age range. This book is particularly useful if parents, caregivers, teachers, and educators participate in the activities with the children. Children have approved all of the techniques, exercises, skills, drills, and active games.

Through creative physical activities and opportunities, I will teach you how to turn your dynamic and hectic lifestyle into a healthy, active one. This series of books, *303 Preschooler-Approved Exercises and Active Games*, *303 Kid-Approved Exercises and Active Games*, and *303 Tween-Approved Exercises and Active Games*, includes more than nine hundred exercises, and each exercise is uniquely designed to fit the needs of a particular age group and has been "kid approved" by the over 75,000 children and teens I have taught throughout my twenty years of teaching fitness. Turn the page to help you turn your child's life into an active life; you have the power to help your children live fit and healthy lives.

Assessing the Needs of Each Child

Kids are naturally active. So what has happened in the last thirty years to change our children's active nature to a sedentary lifestyle in which they are not burning enough of the calories they are consuming? According to Medline Plus, many kids fail to achieve the minimum one hour of physical activity and exercise they need daily, due to overuse of television, video games, and other sedentary activities. Inactive children are more likely to become inactive adults. Kids this age need physical activity to build strength, coordination, and confidence and to lay the groundwork for a healthy lifestyle.

Understanding Children's Health and BMI

Before beginning any exercise program, you (or the parents of your students) should consult a pediatrician to determine each child's current state of health. A pediatrician will address any questions or concerns about a child's health and well-being. If you're concerned that your child is overweight, talk to your pediatrician. Determine if the child is progressing well in relation to basic height and weight categories for their age group. Have a complete understanding of the child's body mass index (BMI). This is a number that is calculated from a child's weight and height; it is age and sex specific. BMI is a reliable indicator of body fat for most children and teens. After BMI is calculated, the number is plotted on a chart with the age and sex of your child to obtain a percentile ranking. The chart shows the weight status categories used with children and teens such as underweight, healthy weight, overweight, and obese.

Addressing the At-Risk or Overweight Child

If a child is overweight, it is something the entire family has to address. Families cannot depend solely on others—day-care providers, babysitters, personal trainers, coaches, and school systems—to provide enough physical activity in a day for children, or to ensure that each child is getting the nutritional food they need in a day from the school cafeteria. There is no question that family behaviors can contribute to childhood obesity and inactive lifestyles. Kids aren't self-sufficient; they are not the ones who shop for food, drive the car to a fast-food restaurant, or set the house rules about how much television they can watch. It is up to the adults to set the guidelines in your family to create an active lifestyle and to provide healthy food choices at home. This task may seem overwhelming, but sometimes it's the smallest decisions that can change a child's life forever.

**Nothing is more important
than the well-being of your child.**

Helping Children Become More Active

Exercise must be an essential part of every child's life. Encouraging regular physical activity is another important thing you can do for the health of your family (as well as your own). Teaching the children around you the importance of being physically active is an invaluable gift to give a child—one that keeps on giving for a lifetime.

Exercise will benefit children by:

- burning calories, which helps in losing or maintaining weight
- helping to strengthen muscles and bones
- improving cardiovascular endurance
- producing endorphins—chemicals that can help children feel more peaceful and happy and can increase self-esteem, mental clarity, and brain function
- reducing the chances of cardiovascular diseases
- decreasing the risk of serious illnesses later in life, including type 2 diabetes and high blood pressure
- reducing the risk of some cancers
- increasing the chances of living longer
- helping increase their creative development
- teaching problem-solving skills
- aiding in motor-skill development
- encouraging family involvement
- improving coordination skills
- assisting in social development
- teaching sportsmanship
- teaching them how to follow basic rules
- teaching them how to receive instruction and direction from someone outside the family
- developing confidence
- developing cognitive thinking
- helping them become more aware of their bodies
- teaching them about caring for their bodies
- helping them sleep well
- providing a healthy appetite
- teaching them become more focused
- helping them establish friendships
- aiding them in developmental growth

Experts recommend that kids six to eight years old get 60 minutes or more of moderate to vigorous physical activity each day. Kids in this age group should not sit inactive for two or more hours.

This physical activity should include aerobic or cardiovascular exercise and muscle-and bone-strengthening exercises. This 60-minute period of time is a minimum, not a maximum, and should be incorporated into a child's day, seven days a week. The 60 minutes of exercise can be broken down into four 15-minute periods of exercise or two 30-minute stretches of exercise, as long as the child receives at least 60 minutes of exercise in total. This exercise can be a structured activity such as soccer, riding a bike, basketball, swimming, dance, gymnastics, or any other heart-pumping sport, or it can be an unstructured activity such as tag, relay races, or any of the other activities described in this book.

Exercise for the Heart and Lungs

Most of the day's physical activity should be composed of either moderate- or vigorous-intensity aerobic physical activity. It is important to understand the definition of "moderate to vigorous physical activity." This refers to the intensity of the energy expenditure. Intensity in exercise is usually described as light, moderate, or vigorous. All levels of intensity will increase your breathing and heart rate, and, as the intensity increases, you should sweat. The higher intensity increases your metabolism, which in turn burns more calories. In addition to burning more calories, your heart becomes stronger just like any other muscle in your body.

For kids, a moderate to vigorous physical activity will increase their breathing and heart rate, and may cause them to sweat. You can teach children about the different levels of intensity by walking. Walk at a slow pace for 10 minutes. Check your heart rate by putting your hand on your heart, counting the number of beats it makes in 10 seconds, and multiplying that by six. That will tell you your heart rate—the number of times your heart beats each minute. Now increase your speed slightly, as if you are running late for an appointment. After 10 minutes you should notice you are breathing harder, your heart rate has increased even more, and you may be perspiring. For vigorous intensity, take your speed to a jog or run. I describe it to kids as imagining that you see a dog just about to run into the street and you want to stop him; that's the pace for vigorous. Your breathing is rapid, but you are still able to talk; you should be able to feel your heart rate without touching your chest; and the top of your head is probably sweaty if beads of perspiration are not dripping down your face. We need our children to work in the moderate to vigorous range.

Exercise for the Muscles and Bones

The heart isn't the only muscle to benefit from regular exercise. Most of the other muscles in the body enjoy exercise, too. When you use your body, your muscles and bones become stronger, and this allows you to be active for longer periods of time without getting worn out. Strong muscles are a plus because they actually help protect you when you exercise by supporting your joints and helping to prevent injuries. Muscles also burn more energy than fat does when a person is at rest, so building your muscles will help you burn more calories and maintain a healthy weight.

For the muscles and joints to move with ease, children need to be flexible. So for any exercise program, they need to learn to stretch. Being flexible may also help your child's sports performance. Some activities, such as dance or martial arts, obviously require great flexibility, but increased flexibility can also help people perform better at other sports, such as football, soccer, or swimming.

For all of these reasons, kids at this age need to exercise, but they do not need formal weight training for building strength. A child's own body weight can help increase strength within their bodies. Many exercises in this book will increase a child's strength. For example, running, jumping rope, and balance exercises are all activities that will help build bone and muscle strength. I recommend that you do the muscle-challenging exercises in this book two to three times a week with this age group. Start slow and select only a couple of exercises; then as the children progress, add more exercises.

The Scoop on Six- to Eight-Year-Olds

For the skills and exercises presented in this book, kids of this age are building on the foundations that were created when they were three to five years old. They are now moving on to more complex movements and skills. They are moving from hitting a ball off a T-ball stand to hitting a ball that is thrown, they are riding a bicycle without training wheels, and, as hand–eye coordination improves, they are catching a ball with one hand and throwing it with the other. Kids at this age may be able to do more than one sport in a day, their endurance levels are increasing, and they can play longer and harder than they were able to at an earlier stage of development. This is the age for instruction and direction; they can actually follow multitask directions and enjoy playing in a group or on a team. This is the time to introduce kids to a variety of sports and to teach them—through skills and drill practice—the sports they like the most.

Kids between six and eight years old are not miniature adults when it comes to an exercise program; they love the fun of a game, the challenge, and practicing a skill that will make them better in their favorite sport. The physical activities in this book offer children all types of physical-fitness components. For instance, if the children choose some of the ball-handling drills, they will be challenging their hearts, muscles, and bones and becoming more flexible as they play. It's easy to fit each type of fitness component into any child's schedule.

—●●●—

Note: For easy reading, we have alternated the use of male and female pronouns. Of course, every "he" also includes "she," and vice versa.

How to Motivate Kids to Be Active—The Secret Is Revealed!

The secret to becoming physically active—which lies within each one of us, young and old—is that we all have something that motivates us. Whether that motivation is the way running makes us feel or the desire to be like our idol, tapping into it is like tapping into super power; it can give us increased energy and make us run farther and jump higher. That motivation—the source of super power—can be either internal or external. The secret to motivating the children in your life to exercise, then, is to find out where their super power comes from and to use this power in every activity.

This super power can be different from one six-year-old to another six-year-old, and each year a child's super power will change, but it is up to you to discover the source of power. Important to that discovery is communication and observation. Begin by asking the children what makes them want to do something. Listen carefully to their answers and then ask why that makes them feel that way. This further questioning may bring out other ideas. Remember to be open-minded about the children's responses.

I discovered this one day when I asked one of my six-year-old students why he liked to exercise. He responded that he wanted to be just like Michael Jordan some day, so he insisted that everyone in our class call him Michael Jordan. Although that wasn't his real name, he was Michael Jordan in his imagination, and that motivated him to jump higher, run faster, and try harder at whatever exercise he was doing in class. Find out who your children's fantasy superhero is and have fun using this to motivate them. Try it yourself: pick an athlete whom you admire and think about how that person would kick a soccer ball or swim laps in a pool.

See what you can observe about the children's motivation, too. If you watch them throughout the day, what external stimulus seems to motivate them to be active? Watch them as they play their favorite games or sports. Keep a list of all motivating factors, no matter how bizarre you think they might be.

- Does music make them move? If so, what type of music?
- Do they seem to take more pleasure from indoor or outdoor activities?
- Are they more active when friends are around them?
- Do they like to set goals for themselves?
- Do they better or more quickly accomplish a goal when a reward system is in place?
- Do professional athletes motivate them?
- Does reading stories in magazines or characters in books motivate them?
- Would a journal or record of their accomplishments keep them on track?
- Do words of encouragement get them moving?
- Would blogging about their accomplishments keep them fired up?
- Do they like the feeling of sweat?
- Would they enjoy an organized team sport?
- Would joining an exercise class help inspire them?
- Do they pride themselves on being unique?
- Are they motivated by other success stories?
- Would before-and-after pictures encourage them?

For years I thought that a video game was the nemesis to an active lifestyle for children. That was until I realized that children's fascination with video games holds other secrets to motivating them to stay active. Watching children play video games has taught me that kids are motivated by:

1. fun
2. competition
3. socialized activities
4. friends and family
5. simple and easy tasks
6. logical and organized thinking experiences
7. variety

8. the enjoyment of the experience

9. positive feedback

10. validation by their peers

Children's fascination with video games holds other secrets about how to motivate them to stay active.

1. Fun Is Not Overrated

Kids are silly and naturally playful; they take play very seriously. Think of the word *play* as an attitude toward life rather than as a form of action. Having a playful attitude toward any activity opens up a world of creative fun. Play is also essential to children's development because it contributes to their cognitive, physical, social, and emotional well-being. Engaging in play can be even more powerful for a child if friends and family members are involved in it.

Make time for play each and every day—even on those days when you think you don't have any time for fun. Exercise should be as fun as you can possibly make it for you and the children around you. It should be an enjoyable experience, so the children keep coming back for more. Go ahead and get creative; you can make anything fun. It can be as simple as asking the children, "How can we make this fun?"

Consider these ideas:

- Do an entire sport skill in reverse.
- Play a game of basketball using only your nondominant hand.
- Play basketball on scooters.
- Make up a game or dance; give it a name.
- Mix it up! Combine two sports into one, swimming/basketball, baseball/soccer, football/ballet, or gymnastics/track.
- Play a game of tag wearing costumes (for example, "Pirate Tag" or "Baby Freeze Tag").

Music can have a profound impact on the mind and on the body. For centuries, music has been used to help heal, calm, motivate, and inspire people. Music can affect the heart rate, breathing patterns, and the mindset in all of us. Music can also make exercising fun. Fitness instructors use music in every classroom situation from yoga to high-impact step classes; the music creates the tempo of movement needed from the students. Selecting the appropriate music for the mood you want to create is the first step. Be sure to choose music that is age appropriate and make sure that the tempo fits a particular exercise. To motivate the children to walk faster, pick music with a faster beat. For yoga, Pilates, and stretching exercises, choose something with a slower tempo.

Finally, create an environment that motivates kids to exercise and makes exercising enjoyable. Designate a space within your home or classroom that has enough room for exercising. Hang some inspirational posters or posters of sport celebrities that may inspire the kids. Consider having basic equipment available. For this age group, big, expensive pieces of equipment are not needed, but below is a list of recommended equipment for your group or family to use for the exercises in this book.

Recommended Fitness Equipment for Kids

- balls of different types
- a basketball hoop
- broomsticks
- cones
- exercise balls
- free weights
- goals
- golf clubs
- jump ropes
- a pitching net
- tennis racquets
- towels
- tubes
- yoga mats

Unstructured, or Free, Play

Kids at this age can't seem to sit still. Their minds are always thinking, and their bodies are always moving. Do not interfere with this stage of discovery. Rather, support it and direct the energy in a positive way, so as to take advantage of your child's natural tendency to be active with unstructured, or free, play.

Unstructured play is vital to a child's physical and mental development. It has no rules or directions to follow; its only limit is the creative reach of your child's imagination. Unstructured play is a powerful activity for all kids because it develops intellectual, emotional, and social skills. But over the last fifteen years, children have begun to spend less time with free play and more time with electronic screen games. Kids need to put away the video games and wake up their imaginations for playtime!

Unstructured activities can be played inside or outside. I recommend that you create a "play space." After all, we have TV rooms, toy rooms, computer rooms, and bedrooms; why not designate a space in your house or a jungle gym in your backyard for fitness? The play space should be a safe environment, attractive to kids, and with enough room and equipment to allow the children to jump, run, tumble, create obstacle courses, and have fun. The equipment, which should be kept in a place where the children can have easy access, can be as simple as mats, balls, and any other objects that will inspire children to get up and move.

And, of course, the best piece of active equipment will be you. Children want and need adults—and specifically parents—to be involved in their world of play.

Note: Although, as noted above, kids from six to eight years old don't spend as much time as they used to engaged in pretend and fantasy games, they do enjoy working on the skills necessary to play their favorite sport. For sport-related games, look in the section on "Sport Fitness" starting on page 103.

2. Add Just the Right Amount of Competition

Competitiveness is a learned behavior. Between the ages of six and eight, kids will experience competition either at home or outside the home. They may pick up a competitive trait from their parents, siblings, teachers, coaches, or from almost any social circumstance. This is a good age to teach children how to keep competition in perspective; with a little direction, they will develop a healthy attitude toward being competitive and have fun with it.

There are various levels of competition, and most depend on the child's age, temperament, culture, sex, and skill level. It's important to realize that some kids at this age thrive on competition, while others become a nervous wreck if they are asked to perform in front of others. This is the perfect time to instill in them that winning isn't everything and that the achievement of a workout or sporting event can be its own merit. Teach children to develop rewards from the inside (from within themselves) and not from the outside; teach them that when they do something right they should tell themselves, "good job." Put in perspective, competitiveness encourages children to work harder and as part of a team, helps them build confidence, and teaches them good sportsmanship by impressing upon them the need to win and lose gracefully.

Children of any age should feel valued regardless of the outcome of any activity. Be careful in your criticism to ensure that it does not appear that your approval and love for your children are dependent on whether they win or lose at a game or other activity. Focus on the process of playing, strategizing, and having fun instead of on the outcome of the activity.

3. Discover Their Identity

At this age, kids begin to tell the world who they are; they are building a sense of identity and self-esteem. It can be a fragile time in their discovery process, so it is important to encourage kids to feel good about themselves. Kids also enjoy being a part of group, sport, or club; or identifying themselves with a sport celebrity. Specific to exercise, kids at this age like to dress the part—maybe dressing like a cyclist or wearing the jersey of their favorite sports team. Adult leaders can use this to their advantage: the more kids think and feel like an athlete, the more fun they will have and the more committed they will be to the sport or exercise.

By implementing a healthy lifestyle when your children are young, you will be raising healthy adults.

4. Involve Friends and Family

Active parents = active kids

As kids' social skills develop, they tend to be more thoughtful and think more about others' reactions. Because of this development, this is the time when kids start to make friends, (although most of their friends are of their same sex at this point). Certainly children of this age group want a parent to be involved in their activities, but by the age of six, friends also begin to become important in kids' lives. So for this age group, involving friends, family, a coach, a personal trainer, or a mentor in creating a healthy lifestyle can provide a great amount of motivation for most kids.

No matter who you choose to partner with a child, you want to make sure that that person has the same or even a greater sense of commitment toward the child's healthy lifestyle as you do. This is important because the habits that are developed in childhood often stay with people throughout their lives. So exercise and active play need to be at the top of your priority list for your child; but it's important to make them a habit and not a chore.

In addition to parents, other family members and older friends automatically become role models for younger children, so we need to live by example. The less you say, the more impact you will have on the children around you. So make physical activity part of your family or group's daily routine. Try playing active games together; it's a great way to combine quality time and an active lifestyle. Or take kids to places where everyone can be active, such as parks, community baseball diamonds, soccer fields, or basketball courts. Miniature golf and batting cages are a lot of fun for everyone, too. Take walks or go for a bike ride; do anything but sit. (Note: And it's especially important to limit "screen" time. Children within this age group should not sit for longer than two hours at a time unless they are sleeping or in school.)

Even household chores are a physical activity—and they teach children responsibility. From toddlers to teens, all children need to learn responsibility by contributing to daily chores and errands. Assigning chores tells them they are a contributor to the family or group and that your family or group works as a team to get things done.

To encourage children to do chores, you need to make the chores fun, so turn tasks into games when possible. Make a chart and give points for putting clothes away. Add a small basketball hoop to the clothes hamper so children can make a basket when they 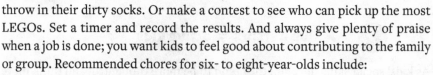 throw in their dirty socks. Or make a contest to see who can pick up the most LEGOs. Set a timer and record the results. And always give plenty of praise when a job is done; you want kids to feel good about contributing to the family or group. Recommended chores for six- to eight-year-olds include:

- carrying out the trash
- helping fold clothes
- helping in the garden
- helping wash the car
- making their own bed
- picking up toys
- putting away their own clothes
- setting and/or clearing the table

- taking care of pets (feeding, helping walk them)
- wiping up the bathroom sink

Note: Although much of the above section refers to the child in the home, these ideas are applicable to/can be adapted for children in group settings such as schools and day cares, too.

5. Simple and Easy Tasks

A child's mind is growing rapidly during these years, so this is a good time to teach them to follow instructions and rules and to practice good sportsmanship.

Follow this procedure with any exercise, game, or activity:

- Make sure you know beforehand how to perform or play the exercise, game, or activity.
- Communicate the rules so that they are simple to follow.
- Be prepared and have all of the equipment you will need.

6. Games and Sports Teach Reasoning and Encourage Thinking

Children of this age group begin to think and reason through situations. Games and exercises can be used to develop and strengthen these skills. Teaching our children new skills from which they will grow can help them develop both physical and mental confidence. And children need to develop competence in movement skills because simpler movements are the building blocks for more complex movements.

To motivate children to be competent, give praise for a job well done and give encouragement at times when children feel they could have done better. Allowing older children to teach younger children how to play a game and allowing children to use their imaginations in games and activities also motivates them.

Games Teach Socialization

Teaching children how to develop relationships may not be something you would normally think about when playing games, but games provide a great opportunity to develop social skills such as sharing, showing respect, supporting teammates, controlling emotions, and more.

Playing a game can do all that and have practical applications as well, such as when you use a name game to introduce one child to another. Game time is also a good time to reinforce listening skills. So, for instance, when one child has a question about a game, be sure that all children listen. And when playing games, de-emphasize winning and competition and emphasize good sportsmanship.

Sports Provide Opportunities to Teach Self-Control

Children at this age have a difficult time controlling their feelings and emotions. Daily practice of a sport or game can help them learn this life skill, as it teaches them discipline. Find the right moments to discuss handling frustration with your children. For example, if a child loses his temper during a game, this is the perfect moment for a conversation on this subject.

Learning the Rules of a New Game Can Teach Focus

Teaching your child how to play a new game can be challenging. Most kids at this age have an attention span of about fifteen minutes, so as adults, we must be creative. First, connect before you direct: Ask all kids to look you in your eyes first and then begin talking to them. Next, as you explain the game, stay brief, stay simple, and ask the kids to repeat your requests back to you. Ask questions to be sure they were listening.

The games that work best for this age group are those that have just a few, simple rules and, preferably, require the children to do only one task at a time.

Since adventure is everything for this age group, learning a new sport or skill can be an easy sell to kids. And the act of learning it teaches kids to conquer fear, set goals, and take risks. If you are unfamiliar with some of the following adventures, research the rules of play, gather your equipment, and have fun.

Individual Sports

- alpine skiing
- archery
- baton twirling
- billiards
- bocce ball
- body surfing
- bowling
- canoeing
- cross-country skiing
- cycling
- dog sledding
- diving
- fishing
- fly-fishing
- golf
- hacky sack
- hang gliding
- hiking/mountaineering

- horseshoes
- ice skating
- Japanese sword arts
- kayaking
- kickboxing
- motocross racing
- mountain biking
- parachuting
- parasailing
- Pilates
- Qi gong
- rafting
- rock climbing
- rollerblading

- rope climbing
- rope jumping
- rowing
- sailing
- scuba diving
- shuffleboard
- skim boarding
- skydiving
- sky surfing
- sledding
- snorkeling
- snowboarding
- snowmobile racing
- snowshoeing

- snow skiing
- speed skating
- surfing
- swimming
- tai chi
- trapeze artistry
- triathlon training and competing
- unicycling
- wake boarding
- water skiing
- weight lifting
- windsurfing
- yoga

Team Sports

- badminton
- baseball
- basketball
- boxing
- broomball
- cheerleading
- cricket
- croquet
- curling
- fencing
- field hockey
- flag football

- football
- handball
- hockey
- hurling
- jai alai
- lacrosse
- laser tag
- lawn bowling
- paintball
- racquetball
- rugby
- soccer

- softball
- squash
- synchronized swimming
- table tennis
- tennis
- ultimate Frisbee
- volleyball
- wrestling

Dance

There are many types of dance:

- ballet
- ballroom
- color guard

- dance sport
- ensemble
- flag twirling

- flamenco
- hip-hop
- interpretive

- jazz
- Latin
- modern
- musical theater
- salsa
- swing
- tango
- tap

Gymnastics

- acrobatic gymnastics
- balance beam
- floor exercises
- high bar
- parallel bars
- pommel horse
- still rings
- trampoline gymnastics
- tumbling
- uneven parallel bars
- vault

Track and Field

- discus
- hammer
- hurdles
- javelin
- jumping events: long jump, triple jump, high jump, pole vault
- relay events
- running events, 5,000- to 10,000-meter races
- shot put
- sprints/dashes 60/100 meter
- 200- to 400-meter races

Martial Arts

Martial means "fighting," but martial arts are art forms that have become sports. Martial arts are rich in tradition; they require discipline and strength from both the mind and the body. While hundreds of different styles of martial arts exist, most are divided into the categories of those involving weapons, hand-to-hand combat, or a combination of the two. The most common martial arts are listed below.

Japanese Martial Arts

- aikido
- judo
- jujutsu (also known as jiu-jitsu)
- karate
- kendo

Korean Martial Arts

- hapkido
- taekwondo

Indian Martial Arts

- Dravidian
- gatka
- kalaripayat
- kuttu varisai
- varma kalai

Brazilian Martial Arts

- capoeira
- Brazillan jiu-jitsu (BJJ)

Chinese Martial Arts

- bagua
- Drunken Boxing
- Eagle Claw
- Five Animals

- Hsing I
- kung fu
- Lau gar
- Monkey

- Praying Mantis
- tai chi chuan
- White Crane
- wing chun

Structured Play

Adults can take cues from the kids as to what activities they'd find most enjoyable and be flexible about trying and learning. Structured play is a physical activity taught in a guided environment, with rules, guidelines, and goals. The American Academy of Pediatrics suggests that team sports are more appropriate for a child six years old and up, while younger children might benefit from a sports class.

7. Variety: Learning Something New Is an Adventure

New experiences are fun waiting to happen. Learning a new sport or activity empowers children to open their minds, meet new people, experience other cultures, challenge their muscles in different ways, and satisfy their desire to be unique.

You can learn a new sport or skill as a family or as part of a group. Try fly-fishing, rock climbing, backpacking, or something simpler like a new yoga move or a new swim stroke. Try snorkeling; if you enjoy it, take a vacation during which your entire family can share in this adventure. But before you set off on that snorkeling trip to Mexico, be sure the children going with you have the skills necessary to be able to snorkel. Consider their age, skill level, and interests.

Through sports and games, children learn about life and the world around them. Games and sports allow children to experience the consequences of their actions; they teach children specific values that can stay with them for the rest of their lives.

Explore the World of Sports and Games

Trying something new creates a unique sense of creativity and adventure. Good things happen when you are not afraid to try. The American Academy of Pediatrics suggests that team sports are appropriate for a child six years old and up. Structured team play:

- teaches a new sport or game
- increases socialization skills
- requires and teaches team-building skills

- teaches responsibility
- teaches a child to focus on specific skills
- requires self-discipline
- develops self-confidence
- teaches the need for showing respect to a coach, other players, and the game
- creates opportunities for children to meet new friends and to challenge themselves
- trains children's muscles for different movements
- teaches children new skills
- presents a unique set of challenging workouts
- presents different workout philosophies (consider karate vs. soccer)
- requires time for training
- teaches new strategies for how to play the game
- trains children to adapt to different situations
- teaches children how to respond in a given situation
- can introduce children to another new sport, such as karate or tai chi

Lifetime Sports

Lifetime sports are any sports or activities that you can play from a very young age and continue playing even as you grow older. It is important to get children involved with some of these sporting activities so they can enjoy physical fitness throughout their lifetimes. Typically these sports are nonimpact, and they are usually easy to find within a community. Examples of lifetime sports include aerobic dance, basketball, boating, bocce ball, bowling, curling, cycling, dance, diving, golf, hiking, lawn bowling, martial arts, racquet sports, running, skating, skiing, snorkeling, swimming, and weight lifting.

8. Enjoyment of the Experience

Because humans are emotional beings, we are driven by how we feel about people, places, and things. What children really want are the feelings of pleasure and satisfaction in the things that they do and accomplish.

All of us are motivated by experiences that make us feel good; most of us will avoid those experiences that make us feel bad or frighten us. As adults we need to keep this in mind when introducing children to new activities. If we see children experiencing fear when faced with a new game, skill, or sport, for instance, we need to look at the situation and figure out why. Perhaps the workout is too hard or too competitive. Is there a risk involved? Does the child think it may make her look foolish to her friends? Whatever the fear might be, you must identify it; once the fear is gone or overcome, then the children can focus on the fun of the activity.

You can alleviate some fear by always making safety a priority in any workout. This includes making sure the workout is age and skill appropriate for the children. Check all equipment or toys that will be used to ensure that they are safe to use. Always have a responsible adult supervising all activities.

Reward System

Celebrate success! Even if the success is marking only baby steps, it is a step in the right direction. A reward system can make a workout more enjoyable. If children know what is expected of them and they accomplish the goal, it's great to receive some form of a reward. A reward system must be a positive experience.

To encourage a healthy lifestyle, don't offer rewards such as food, beverages, or trips to favorite restaurants. Food should never be a reward; it sends the wrong message, especially if children are trying to lose weight. Never withhold food as a punishment either. Neither use of food sends the message we want children to hear, so, it is best to offer nonfood items as rewards. Consider rewards such as:

- achievement certificates to mark minor or major achievements in your healthy lifestyle program (children can collect these awards and put them in a box or a scrapbook)
- a gold star program that is similar to the achievement certificates, but the gold stars are displayed so everyone can see them
- ribbons, trophies, certificates, movie passes, books, manicures, pedicures, new workout clothes, facials, foot massages at a spa or a spa day, a day at the beach or a favorite park, a picnic, a special outing, a new piece of exercise equipment

You might also ask the children for some ideas for rewards. Be sure to write down any ideas they give you and save them for future reference.

Make sure any rewards are age appropriate.

9. Results and Feedback

When working with children, you want to build pride, confidence, and muscle all at the same time. In the pursuit of healthy children, look past the pursuit of a healthy body; it is also the pursuit of a healthy mind. To raise a well-balanced child, you can't have one without the other.

A positive message stimulates and empowers anybody, especially kids. Words have power; they can build someone up or they can tear someone down. So especially when working with children, you want to choose your words carefully and think about the value and delivery of your feedback. Positive reinforcement can increase self-confidence, so give children personal compliments. Also make sure to give specific feedback; this increases the value of the statement.

In regard to how you say something, be genuine about your comments. If you are struggling for something good to say and you are fake or phony with your feedback, the kids will see right through your comment and your feedback will lose authenticity. Don't offer a compliment followed by the word *but*; they won't hear anything you say before that word. Express how their efforts or behaviors affected others, "Your strong commitment to hockey makes you a great role model for your younger brother!" Use only encouraging words to correct a skill. To change or implement a desirable behavior, use cues and positive reinforcement to direct a child toward a specific behavior. In addition, know what motivates a specific child—particularly your own.

10. Validation

Feelings of acceptance and validation must start at home. Children have a strong need for love and understanding from their parents as well as their peers. Kids want and need their parents' attention and approval. We all possess the desire to do something or be someone that is valued or valuable. Some children have the desire to be like others, while others strive to be unique. One thing that is common in children is that no child likes to be compared to another child in a negative way.

Find the strengths within the individual child and develop them but don't push a child into a sport or activity because you played it as a child or because a friend's children are involved in it now. If a child does not want to play on an organized team, don't push them in that direction. Instead, explore the list of individual sports mentioned in this book with your children. Maybe skateboarding is more their style. Or if children want to be different, let them try a sport that is not common, such as fencing or an Indian martial art.

Nuts and Bolts: The Exercises in This Book

The exercises described in the remainder of this book have been "kid ap-proved." These are the exercises I have used for personal training sessions, kids fitness classes, kids fitness camps, birthday parties, and in-school ses-sions. Kids enjoy these exercises. Some may seem silly or too easy to adults. But remember: These exercises are for six- to eight-year-old kids; they are de-signed for their muscles, skill level, and coordination.

How to Use the "Kid-Approved" Exercises

What exercise is best for your child? The answer is whatever exercise they like best. Favorite physical activities might be part of the school setting during ex-tracurricular activities, or they might be played at home where parents and or grandparents can take part as leaders and coaches. It is important for adults to play an accepting and encouraging role in to lead kids to a healthier lifestyle.

No matter what activities you and the children choose, some guidelines apply to them all. Following are some thoughts to help get you started.

Safety Comes First

Safety should be a number-one concern when exercising, and a few basic ideas about that are appropriate to any and every game or activity:

- Be sure that the play area is free of electrical cords, sharp objects, or anything that may harm the children.
- If equipment is needed, be sure it is age appropriate and that the chil-dren know how to use each piece correctly.
- Keep children hydrated even in cooler temperatures.
- Make sure the children are wearing clothing appropriate for the weather.
- Don't forget to apply (and reapply) sunscreen.
- Most important: Make sure the children are supervised in any activity.

Some safety issues apply to specific sports and activities. For instance, helmets are needed for sports such as baseball, football, softball, biking, snow sports, and rollerblading. It is important that your kids wear the right helmet for the sport that they are playing. The helmet should have a sticker from the Consumer Product Safety Commission (CPSC), which designates that it is safe wear for a particular activity, such as biking.

Other safety pieces include mouth guards, body pads, and eye gear. If children are playing any activity in which there is a chance of getting hit in the head or, specifically, the face, they need to get and use mouth guards. You can get mouth guards from a dentist or a sporting goods store. Elbow, knee, and wrist pads should be worn when skateboarding, snowboarding, skating, or playing ice hockey to help protect against broken bones. And special eye protection may be needed for sports such as ice hockey, lacrosse, and racquetball. Make sure the goggles and face masks fit snuggly against the face.

Make Exercise Fun

Choose exercises from each category—warm-up and stretching, mind and body, strength, cardiovascular exercises, and active games, sport challenges, and drills. Put them together in one of the formats listed below.

Circuit Training

This type of workout combines different exercises into one workout. It is very easy to create your own circuit training routine. To begin, select 8 to 10 different exercises from this book. Write the name and description of each exercise on a separate index card. Collect any equipment you may need for the exercises you've chosen.

Spread all of the exercise cards on the floor in a large circle, with each card marking a "station." The area must be large enough for each participant to have room to perform each exercise. Tell the kids to choose one station to begin with; it is best if only one player is at each station. Set a time allowance for each round of exercises. When the time is up, each participant moves one station to the right and begins to perform the exercise on that particular card.

Examples of Circuit Training

- baseball-stations circuit
- body-part circuit
- boys-only circuit
- girls-only circuit
- healthy-heart circuit
- indoor circuit

- outdoor circuit
- soccer-stations circuit
- stations-that-use-balls circuit

Interval Training

Add a cardiovascular activity to repeat in between each station. For example, choose from:

- hopping on one leg
- jumping
- leg kicks (forward, backward, side to side)
- running (forward, backward, sideways)

Participants perform the cardio exercise for a predetermined period of time (for example, three minutes) and then go right into the movements you have selected for the next station.

Sports Theme

Select a sport and then select a list of exercises from this book that would fit the theme of that sport.

Backward Activities

Choose a list of movements and perform all of the activities backward.

Theme Day

Choose a theme and wear a relevant costume while the performing the games and exercises that reflect that theme.

Pyramid Style

Start with one card. When you have completed the movements, add two more cards. Repeat the movements from the beginning. Next, add three more cards to the routine. Repeat all of the exercises from the beginning.

Choreograph

Link a variety of moves together to create a choreographed routine. You can even add music to the workout.

Vacation

If your family is planning an outdoor adventure such as skiing, kayaking, hiking, or swimming, use that adventure as your theme. Choose exercises and games that will help prepare the muscles to be used during your adventure. Be sure to take along this book to keep your family in shape while you travel.

Attend a Baseball, Football, Basketball, or Soccer Game

Taking kids to a ball game can be very exciting for the entire family or group. You can increase the excitement by focusing on the sport skills for those particular sports before and after the visit to the game. Practice some of the applicable drills listed in this book. Let your children see how the exercises they have been doing really do apply to a ball game.

Birthday Party Games

Birthday party games are one of the most important parts of the party. Oh the cake, ice cream, and presents are fun, too, but if you don't have a way to entertain the party guests, it can quickly turn into a whiny or out-of-control party.

The games included in this book are easy to follow with a minimum of supplies, and they all will ensure lots of laughs from the guests. Parties should be fun, and these games help make that fun happen.

Create a Fitness Plan

It's not enough for kids to know that they should be exercising to keep their bodies healthy. Sometimes it takes the planning of a fitness program from an adult to keep kids on track with exercise.

When planning any exercise program, choose a group of activities based upon a bell-shaped curve. Look at the activities that you have planned and place them in order of energy expenditure. Start off with activities that will get the children moving but won't exhaust their energy levels from the beginning. Next add on another activity that requires more energy. At the peak of the bell-shaped curve, select the activity with the highest level of energy expenditure. Follow that with activities that gradually decrease energy expenditure until it is time to wrap out the session with some cool-down stretches.

The following are some examples of exercise plans. Kids can have short attention spans, so you want to be prepared with many activities for them to do. Each list of activities takes approximately 30 to 45 minutes to complete. Be sure to gather all of the equipment you will need for your program before you start.

Example Number One (60 Minutes)

1. Running in Place (#119)
2. ten stretches (#1–10)
3. a game to get the kids excited and have them interact with other kids (#232, #253, #254)
4. fitness skills, such as jumping (#120, #124, #130)
5. one race (#290, #293, #294)

6. an obstacle course, combination of exercises (#103, #136, #137, #233)

7. three strength-building exercises (#52, #61, #74)

8. three balance activities (#173, #176, #177)

9. yoga postures do one set of each of these postures (#27, #29, #30, #31, #32, #34, #36, #51, #56, #57)

10. Graveyard Game (#254), for a cool down

Example Number Two (30 Minutes)

- Running in Place (#119)
- five stretches (#2, #4, #5, #7, #8)
- five exercises to develop muscle strength (#58, #60, #71, #89, #92)
- two fine motor skill exercises (#188, #189)
- one tag game (#273, #278, #281)
- one mind and body exercise (#30, #31, #34, #51)

Example Number Three (30 Minutes)

- Running in Place (#119)
- three cardio exercises (#120, #122, #136)
- five stretches (#1, #3, #4, #5, #8)
- five strength-building exercises (#58, #129, #131, #136, #137)
- three running games (#290, #273, #296)
- three sport skills (#191, #192, #194)

When adding physical activity to children's daily routines, start slowly. The following are some examples of how you can incorporate physical activity into activities that may already be part of those routines.

- play a favorite sport: 30 minutes + 10 minutes stretching
- tackle household chores: 30 minutes + 10 minutes stretching + 15 minutes sport drills
- walk: 30 minutes + 10 minutes outdoor meditation + 15 minutes stretching outdoors
- shoot baskets: 30 minutes + 15 minutes stretching + 15 minutes strength training
- bicycle: 30 minutes + 15 minutes Pilates + 15 minutes meditation
- dance: 30 minutes + 15 minutes stretching + 15 minutes strength training

- play in the pool: 30 minutes + 30 minutes strength training
- jump rope: 15 minutes + 15 minutes upper-body exercises (#58, #61, #72, #74)
- play a game: 60 minutes + 10 minutes stretching + 15 minutes sport drill (#191)
- watch television: 30 minutes + 15 minutes of sport drills + 15 minutes of cardiovascular exercises (#120, #127, #136)
- eat dinner: 30 minutes + 30 minutes walking + 10 minutes meditation (see page 45)

Partner Training

Training with a partner can be fun and motivating. Most of the exercises in this book that are designed for pairs can be used for either child/child or adult/child partners. So, if you are working with your own children, you can choose a group of activities that allow you to spend quality time with your children and get in a good workout.

As another option, get a group of family members or friends to exercise along with you. You can even design programs for each other.

Personal Training

The objective of hiring a personal trainer is to have a customized program that is right for your children. With over three hundred exercises in this book, customizing a program for an individual or group is easy. All of these exercises have been used with kids for years; just read through each exercise and pick the right ones for your situation. The rule of thumb is that if your children want to lose weight, you should add more cardiovascular exercises to the program. To strengthen muscle, select from the exercises for the torso, upper body, and lower body. To improve speed, endurance, and coordination, try sport skills and drills. Always have the children warm-up before exercise, add stretching, add strength training, include yoga or Pilates, and have fun customizing the program.

Here is a sample daily exercise plan. It uses a combination of cardiovascular exercises and body-weight resistance training:

Daily Training Guide
Day 1: Upper-body training + meditation
Day 2: Cardiovascular workout + yoga
Day 3: Lower-body and core/torso training + Pilates
Day 4: Cardiovascular workout + stretching
Day 5: Upper-body training + Pilates

Day 6: Cardiovascular workout + yoga

Day 7: Game day

Keeping a Fitness Journal

Keeping a fitness journal is another way to keep children motivated, so have each participant keep a journal. (You may have to help the younger children with their entries.) Explain the benefits of keeping a journal and give the children some ideas about the detail that can be kept in them, including:

- Logging the minutes of a weekly workout plan. Seeing the time add up can help boost motivation. Set up a contract with the children that offers rewards for racking up minutes.

- Noting challenges to peers or family members on number of repetitions.

- Tracking personal best times or noting your accomplishments in each fitness category. Have the children keep track of and then try to beat their old records. Recording their progress allows them to see and feel the achievements.

Here is an example of a fitness journal:

Daily Progress Report   Date: _____

Upper-Body Exercises

Time to complete: ____ or number of repetitions: _____

1. (List exercises)
2.
3.
4.
5.

Cardiovascular Exercises

1.
2.

Time to complete: _____

Number of repetitions: ____

Obstacle Course

You and the children can create your own obstacle course by selecting some of the exercises from this book, writing the names and descriptions on index cards, and placing the cards at stations inside or outside of your meeting space or home. Transform the yard, living room, or other area into a free-for-all obstacle course. Remove unsafe objects from the area. Collect any equipment you may need to complete the course, such as balls, a mini-trampoline, etc., beforehand. Challenge children to navigate their way through the series of exercises while being timed. Record all results and encourage participants to try to beat their own best time.

Races and Relay Races

Races are great exercise whatever your age. When engaged in a race, not only does a child get their heart pumping but the child also has to learn that even in the emotional excitement of an intense game or close race, she has to observe rules and regulations; to choose between fair or unfair, and to act on those choices appropriately.

When you have a larger group of kids (10 players or more), relay races keep the pace of the game moving. During a relay race, each team member participates in only a set part of the race, and he then tags another member of the team to continue the game until each player has had a turn.

Select any of the cardiovascular exercises in this book. Identify the starting line and the finish line. On "Go," each player must perform the movement as fast as he can all the way to the finish line.

Pyramid Style

Select a series of approximately fifteen exercises. Have the children perform the first exercise. Then add on the next exercise and repeat the sequence from the beginning. Add on a third exercise and repeat from beginning. Add on exercises until the full sequence includes all of the chosen exercises.

Choreograph

Link chosen exercises together to create a choreographed routine. Add music to the workout to further inspire the participants.

Drills to Increase Sports Performance

Select a series of drills with which children can challenge a friend or family member.

As they approach eight years old, children begin to enjoy learning new skills and sports. This is a good time to introduce lifetime sports such as dance, swimming, tennis, golf, and martial arts.

Exercising in Hot or Cold Weather

During hot weather, it's important to prevent children from getting overheated and dehydrated. Young children are in more danger of both for several reasons. They have a greater surface-area-to-body-mass ratio than adults, so they absorb more heat from the sun and air. And because they don't sweat as much, they produce more heat, so they don't cool off as well. Similarly, on a cold day, they have a greater heat loss than adults.

On top of these physical differences, kids take playing games very seriously, so they aren't aware that they need to take a break and drink water. Children with certain medical conditions, including obesity, diabetes, and heart disease, are at even greater risk for overheating and dehydration.

It is recommended to postpone or minimize strenuous activity when heat and humidity are high and to make sure the children are taking in plenty of fluids before, during, and after exercise. Have them drink 4 to 8 ounces of fluid 30 minutes before an activity, another 4 to 8 ounces every 20 to 30 minutes during the activity, and 4 to 8 ounces after the activity.

On especially hot and humid days, have children spend as much time indoors as possible. If your home does not have air conditioning, take them to a public place like a shopping mall to walk around. Schedule outdoor activities during the coolest times of the day so children don't spend too much time in the sun, and slow the activities down. Make sure children are wearing appropriately lightweight clothing, a hat, and sunscreen. Use a spray mister to cool down active children, and, if they get too heated, have them take cool baths or showers.

Why These Exercises Were Chosen

When it comes to fitness, children are not miniature adults. Children have specific physiologic differences that make them unique. Therefore, their fitness programs, exercises, and activities must be specific to their developmental stage and not just a watered-down version of an adult's. For example, children of this age do not need exercises for building tight abdominal muscles or increasing the size of their biceps.

The exercises in this book were chosen because they are safe for most kids within this age group. They were also chosen because they challenge children's minds and bodies in fun and creative ways. Kids are the teachers when it comes to having fun, and the kids designed these "fun ways." Kids will repeat an activity that is fun, creative, and makes them feel good. The physical activities involved in this book are a combination of high- and low-intensity movements. These challenge children's muscular and cardiovascular strength and endurance.

You can turn these exercises into playful competitions and/or challenges. Playful competition challenges kids to work harder against themselves or other players. It also involves skill development, increases focus, and challenges kids to think smarter by developing creative strategies and tactics for succeeding.

Rules of Training

Always start with a warm-up. Prior to doing any of the exercises in this book, you should have participants do exercises that gradually elevate body temperature, heart rate, and loosen muscles for the workout ahead. Read the section entitled "Stretching and Flexibility Exercises" starting on page 36 and then choose the stretches that you think the children will like for each part of the body.

Start slowly. Over time, gradually increase the amount of time the children exercise.

Perform each exercise slowly. When children are learning a new exercise or, perhaps, coming back from an illness, it is important to perform each exercise slowly. When they perform an exercise too quickly, they are using momentum and not muscle strength. By taking an exercise slowly, children are less likely to experience injury, too.

Stretching exercises can be done every day. Teach children to ease into each stretch slowly until they feel the muscles and connective tissues being stretched. They should then hold the stretch and breathe. Hold each stretch for a slow count of 15.

Vary the exercises. To avoid boredom and to challenge the body, change the exercises every four weeks.

Note: Sitting and Standing Exercises

Unless otherwise designated, participants should keep their feet hip-distance apart. If the exercises call for sitting on a chair, children's feet should touch the ground. For shorter children whose feet are unable to reach the floor, add a stack of books. Each participant's hands should rest on his thighs or at the side of his body.

To help children find the best posture, have them follow you through this exercise. First round your back slightly, tilting your pelvis forward and flattening the small curve in your back. Then tilt your pelvis backward, creating an exaggerated curve in your back. Now find the neutral position somewhere between these two positions. Be sure to pull your belly button back toward your spine in each exercise to engage abdominal or stomach muscles. Maintain this natural curve of the spine in each exercise. Engaging the stomach muscles this way will help support the back muscles.

Proper alignment. Show the children the proper alignment for each stretching exercise, including maintaining a neutral alignment with the spine, keeping the belly button pulled back toward your spine, and keeping the head aligned with the spine. Remind all participants to breathe throughout each exercise.

Key to the Icons Used in the Games

To help you find games suitable for a particular situation, the games included in this book are coded with symbols or icons. These icons tell you, at a glance, the following specifics about the game:

- the size of the group needed
- if a large space is needed
- if physical contact is or might be involved
- if participants will exercise on a mat
- if props are required
- if music is required

These icons are explained in more detail below. Two of the icons included in other SmartFun books—those for "age level" and "time"—have been omitted because the games presented here are categorized by skill level rather than age level and because the duration of each game will vary depending on a number of factors, including the size of the group, the physical activity involved, the time limit set by the leader, variations or modifications made by the leader, and whether the particular game appeals to the players.

The size of the group needed. Most of the activities may be performed with groups of any size. A few are designed for pairs, small groups, or the whole group. These exceptions are individually marked with one of the following group-size icons:

 = The whole group plays together.

 = Participants play individually, so any size group can play.

 = Participants play in small groups of three or more.

 = Participants play in pairs.

If a large space is needed: A large space is required for some of the games, such as when the whole group is required to form a circle or to walk around the room. These are marked with the following icon:

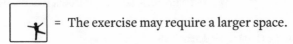 = The exercise may require a larger space.

If physical contact is or might be involved: Although a certain amount of body contact might be acceptable in certain environments, the following icon has been inserted at the top of any games that definitely involves contact or might involve anything from a small amount of contact to minor collisions. You can figure out in advance if the game is suitable for your participants and/ or environment.

 = Physical contact is involved or likely.

If an exercise mat is required: Many of the exercises in this book should be done on an exercise mat.

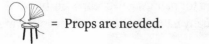 = Players will exercise on mats.

If props are required: Many of the games require no special props. In some cases, though, items such as balls, jump ropes, chairs, or other materials are integral to running and playing a game. Games requiring props are flagged with the icon below, and the necessary materials are listed under the Props heading. Note that optional props will also be flagged.

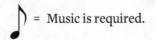 = Props are needed.

If music is required: Only a few games in this book require recorded music. If the music is optional, it is noted as such. In either case, the icon below is used:

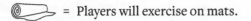 = Music is required.

The Exercises
and Games

Stretching and Flexibility Exercises

Except
as noted

Warming up is an essential part of any exercise routine and should never be forgotten. A warm-up exercise increases blood flow to the working muscles and prepares the body for the movements ahead. To get started, have participants spend 5 minutes on the warm-up activities listed below and then move onto stretching exercises.

Warm-Up Activities

A proper warm-up can increase the blood flow to the working muscle, which results in decreased muscle stiffness, less risk of injury, and improved performance. Additional benefits of warming up include physiological and psychological preparation.

Breathing

Teach children to always begin an exercise routine by increasing their breath. Have them follow your lead. Inhale deeply through your nose and exhale all the air from your lungs out of your mouth. Try this at least 5 times. If anyone starts to feel light-headed, stop and resume regular breathing. To increase energy in the body, have the kids try this deep breathing several times throughout the day. If they feel stress or want to relax at the end of the day, have them focus on the exhaling part of this breath work.

Slow Dancing

The first part of the warm-up should be moving each part of the body very slowly. Have the children follow your lead as you start with your head and move down to your toes, working every part of your body. Roll your head from side to side. Roll your shoulders up, down, and in circles front and back. Swing your arms in a circle and then reverse the direction. Be sure to include bending your elbows and moving your fingers. Slowly twist your torso from one side to the other side. Swing your arms gently overhead and then down toward the floor, bending your knees and slightly leaning forward. Keep taking deep breaths throughout your slow dance. Step forward, backward, and side to side. Rotate your ankles and wiggle your toes.

Marching in Place

With the children following your lead, begin by taking a deep breath in through your nose. Exhale through your mouth. Begin to march lightly in place. Gradually lift your knees higher. Keep your head lifted and shoulders pulled back.

Walking

Lead the children on a walk anywhere outside or inside. You can even walk in place.

Light Jogging

As a warm-up exercise, a light jog will help increase the blood flow to the working muscles. Lead the children as you increase your speed slightly toward the end of your 7-minute warm-up.

Shuffling

Lead the children in a shuffle step. Begin with your feet together then, without lifting your right foot off the floor, slide it out to your right side and then slide your left foot to the right to meet it, also without lifting your foot off the floor. Repeat this shuffle step 8 times to your right side and then 8 times to your left side. Your body should feel warm and ready for exercise, and your mind should be clear of thoughts. Your group should be ready for the workout ahead.

Stretching Exercises

Children are flexible at this age. But even with their flexibility, it is extremely important to warm up the muscles they will be using before any exercise. Stretching reduces the chances of injury and establishes a good foundation before any physical activity.

 **Demonstrate each exercise first.
Then teach the children how to perform it.**

Stretching is good for any body; it helps to prepare the muscles, tendons, and ligaments for an activity. Being flexible helps prevent injuries, and your body recovers better after an exercise. If you stretch, it helps reduce muscle tension and stiffness. Perform each stretching activity, letting the children follow your lead. Hold the positions for 10 to 15 seconds.

Neck Stretch

Tell the children: Sit or stand with your chin slightly tucked to your chest. Turn your head slowly to bring your chin to one shoulder, hold for three seconds, and then turn to the other shoulder. Repeat 5 times and breathe throughout.

Shoulder Rolls

Tell the children: Rotate your shoulders as big as you can 5 times in one direction. Then reverse the direction of the rolls and rotate your shoulders 5 times.

Shoulder-Blade Rolls

Tell the children: With your elbows bent behind your body, roll your shoulders back until the shoulder blades come as close together as possible. Press shoulder blades together for 5 breaths. Repeat this 10 times.

Arm Circles

Tell the children: Stretch your arms out to your sides at shoulder height. Begin circling the arms in one direction 10 times and then reverse directions for 10 times. Create both big and small circles.

Hug Yourself

Tell the children: Wrap your arms around your body and give yourself a big hug. This is great to do every day!

Shoulder Shrugs

Tell the children: Inhale and lift your shoulders up toward your ears. Exhale and slowly lower your shoulders back down. Repeat 10 times and then alternate shoulders, raising one at a time.

Superman Stretch

Tell the children: In a standing position, place your hands on your hips and pull your shoulders back as far as they will go. Keeping your shoulders pressed down, you should feel a stretch in your chest. Hold this stretch for 15 seconds.

Fold Yourself in Half

Tell the children: From a standing position, bend forward and try to touch your toes. You will feel this stretch in the back of your legs. Hold this stretch for 15 seconds.

Cat and Cow

Tell the children: Stand with feet hip-width apart, bend forward and place hands right above your knees. Round your back upward toward the sky and pull your belly button in toward your spine. Count to 15 and release, letting your body sag slightly to stretch in the opposite direction.

Overhead

Tell the children: In a standing position, extend your arms up and over your head, holding your hands together. Hold this stretch for 15 seconds.

Back Stretch

Tell the children: Beginning in a standing position, slowly roll your back down from the bottom to the top of your spine all the way until you reach your tailbone. Hold this position for 15 seconds, allowing your arms to hang. Then slowly roll back up into a standing position.

Butterfly Wings

Tell the children: Sitting on the floor with your knees together, place both hands around your ankles. Slowly lower your knees out to the sides as far as they can go and hold the position for 15 seconds. As you breathe, slowly bring your knees back together.

 ## Smell Your Stinky Toes

Tell the children: In a seated position with knees pointing out to each side, bring the bottoms of your feet together. Hold both feet with your hands and lean over from the waist, trying to touch your nose to your toes. Hold and breathe. Repeat 5 times.

 ## Knee to Chest

Tell the children: Lie on your back with both feet flat on the floor. Bring your left knee into your chest and give it a hug. Hold, breathe, and count to 15. Return that leg to the floor and repeat the stretch with the other leg.

 ## Walk on Heels

This is a great exercise for stretching the calf muscle and for balance.

    Tell the children: Begin walking on the heels of your feet. Walk this way for 30 seconds.

 ## Walk on Toes

Tell the children: In a standing position, raise yourself up onto your toes, heels lifted off the floor, and walk around for 30 seconds.

17   Ankle Circles

Props   A chair or a mat for each participant

Tell the children: Sit on a chair or lie on your back on the floor. Bring your right knee up toward your chest. Circle the ankle to the right and then to the left. Lower this leg and repeat the movement with the other ankle.

18   Swan Stretch

Tell the children: Kneel on the ground and sit back on your heels, keeping your back straight. Lean back, bringing your arms forward to help with balance. Hold this position. Now reverse the position by bringing your upper body forward and extending your arms straight out behind your back. Hold and breathe.

19   Inner-Thigh Stretch

Tell the children: Stand with your feet about 2–3 feet apart and toes facing forward. Bend your left knee, making sure your left knee doesn't move forward beyond your left toes. Rotate your pelvis slightly to the left to increase the stretch of your right inner thigh.

Feel the stretch in the inner thigh and hold it for 15 seconds. Then switch legs and repeat.

20   Upright-Spine Twists

Props   A chair or a mat for each participant

Tell the children: This twist is done in a seated position with your spine lengthened. Keeping your hips straight ahead and your arms folded across your chest, rotate your shoulder back as far as you can without moving your hips; allow your head to follow. Breathe and hold for 15 seconds. Return to the center and take 5 deep breaths. Rotate to your left side, breathe, and hold. Repeat sequence 3 times.

21 Spinal Twists

Tell the children: Lie on your back with your arms at your sides, your feet flat on the floor, and your knees together. Slowly drop your knees to your left side, keeping your shoulders on the floor. Hold this for 15 seconds and then bring your knees back to center. Slowly drop your knees to your right side, breathe, and hold for 15 seconds.

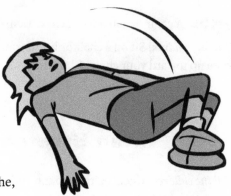

22 Full-Body Stretch

Tell the children: This is a great stretch to do before you jump out of bed in the morning. Lie on your back with legs long. Stretch both arms overhead for 15 seconds. Pretend as if someone is pulling your arms in one direction and your feet in the opposite direction.

23 Quadriceps Stretch

Props A wall or a chair for each participant

Tell the children: In a standing position, hold on to a wall or chair with your left arm, grab your right ankle, and bring your heel toward your bottom. Hold the stretch in the front of the thigh for 15 seconds. Repeat this stretch using your other leg and arm.

Partner Stretches

The following stretches are done with the help of a partner.

24   Chest Stretch

Divide the group into pairs or have the players choose partners.

Tell the children: Partners stand facing away from each other with the same foot forward and the same foot back. Extend arms behind your bodies and grab onto each other's hands. Breathe and bend your front knee forward slightly to lean away from each other. Hold the stretch for 15 seconds and repeat 3 times.

25   Straddle Stretch

Divide the group into pairs or have the players choose partners.

Tell the children: Work in pairs. Sit facing your partner with your legs spread apart in a straddle position. Lean forward to grab each other's hands. Have your partner place his feet on the inside of your leg. Lean back to pull your partner forward, bending so his arms are straight. Hold for 15 seconds and repeat 3 times. Then switch roles.

26   Supported Cat

Divide the group into pairs or have the players choose partners.

Tell the children: Work in pairs. Have one partner start on all fours. The other partner stands, with his legs straddling the first player's legs. The standing partner then places his hands under the other player's waist, who then rounds her back upward, and lowers her head, letting the standing partner pull her up a little more. Hold the position for 15 seconds; repeat 3 times.

Mind and Body Exercises

Stress is a part of everyone's lives, including those of our children. We experience stress from three different sources: our bodies, our thoughts, and our environment. As children grow older, they will face various levels of stress. We can help them by recognizing when they are feeling stress and teaching them techniques that can help reduce it.

Progressive relaxation can be practiced lying down or in a chair with your head supported. Each muscle group is contracted and held in a tense state for 5 to 7 seconds and then relaxed.

In the beginning, it is important to lead the children, announcing which body part they should squeeze and then relax before moving on to the next body part. I prefer to start at the top of the head and work my way down to the toes. Tell the children to close their eyes, listen to your voice, and squeeze each part of the body you identify. Explain that they will hold the squeeze for 5 to 7 seconds and then relax that part of the body.

Begin by having the children clear their heads of any tension or bad thoughts. Tell them to visualize the tension and thoughts leaving the head. Now, starting at the top of the body, identify major muscles. Have the children squeeze their foreheads, mouths, jaws, shoulders, backs, and arms (one at a time), and so on. After some practice, the kids will learn to do the entire sequence on their own.

Breathing Techniques

Proper breathing habits are essential for good mental and physical health. Teach the children to breathe deeply in through their noses and exhale through their mouths. Have them take deeps breaths and shallow breaths, close off one nostril and breathe, and then switch nostrils.

To help the children understand better breathing techniques, have them lie down on the floor, in a "dead body pose." Lead the group, showing them how you place one hand on your stomach and one hand on your chest. Inhale slowly and deeply through your nose; feel your hand being pushed up and watch as your chest moves in opposition of your stomach.

Meditation and Visualization

In other parts of the world, it is common to see children practice meditation, but here in the United States it is a practice that only recently has been accepted into our lifestyles. Meditation can be a healthful way of learning to control thoughts, anger, stress, sadness, and any issues that may be troubling us, or it can be just a chance to sit back and absorb the world around us.

To practice meditation, it is important to make an environment that is free from distractions such as televisions, cell phones, and computers. The space doesn't have to be large; so you can even create your own meditation spot in your bedroom.

To begin meditation, start in a relaxed posture. This can be sitting in a cross-legged position, sitting in a comfortable chair, or lying down on a mat on the floor. It is not recommended that you lie on your bed because you may fall asleep. You should meditate every day, starting with 5-minute sessions and working up to 30 minutes. Meditation is a great way to get children of this age to relax a little more easily.

Close your eyes gently and take several deep breaths. As you inhale, feel the air coming into your lungs; as you exhale, release any stress you may have in your body. Notice your thoughts, and as they enter your mind, acknowledge them and visualize them leaving your body.

AHHHHHH.

We all sigh once or twice during the day without even realizing it. This is our body's way of increasing oxygen to the brain and relaxing the body.

Stress and Anger

Stress and anger happen to all of us—even children. It is important to teach kids how to control and reduce their frustrations. When a child is upset, remove her from the situation if needed; instruct her to take 5 deep breaths, close her eyes, squeeze and relax tense muscles, and use words only to describe how and why she is feeling tension.

See This

To teach your children how to visualize during meditation, have them sit in a comfortable position. Ask them to close their eyes, take several deep breaths, and picture in their minds items that they can easily identify: an orange, an apple, a sunny day, a yellow smiley face, a gold star. This may take some time for them to see these items in their minds, but with practice, it will become easier.

Taste This

Ask the children to close their eyes, take several deep breaths, and imagine a series of items their taste buds can easily identify, such as tartness of a green apple, the sweetness of honey, the cold feeling of an ice cube, or the warm sensation of a bowl of oatmeal. Try to use healthy foods instead of junk foods.

Smell This

Ask the children to close their eyes, take several deep breaths, and picture in their minds items that their noses can easily identify, such as the smell of cinnamon rolls, cookies baking, a pizza, air after a rainfall, or freshly laundered sheets.

Feel This

Ask the children to close their eyes, take several deep breaths, and picture in their minds items that they can easily identify by the sense of touch, such as a cotton ball, a bunny, a soft pillow, a sharp pin, a hug, an icy snowball, or a warm fireplace.

Journal

Teach the children to record their experiences and insights about their daily life in the journals they have started (see page 29). Suggest that they record any feelings—good or bad—and reassure them that this journal is private unless they feel like sharing their writings with someone.

Core Strengthening

Except
as noted

All of our movements are powered by our torso, or core—it is the body's center of power. The abs and back work together to support the spine when we sit, stand, bend over, pick things up, and exercise.

27 Child's Pose

Tell the children: Kneel down. Keeping your neck in a neutral position, fold over at the waist and stretch your arms out in front of you. Relax and breathe. Use this posture whenever you need to rest from other yoga postures and remain in this posture until you feel ready to move on.

28 Tabletop

Tell the children: Start out on all fours. Slide your right leg behind you and lift it to hip height. Do not sink into your left hip; keep your hips parallel with the floor. Slide your left arm out in front of you, keeping your palm facing the floor. Keep your head and neck in alignment with your spine. Lift your left arm to shoulder height. Hold the pose for 10 breaths. Slowly lower your arm and then your leg to the floor. Hold for 10 breaths. Repeat 5 times. Repeat this posture with your other arm and leg.

Long Neck

Tell the children: Stand with your feet hip-distance apart, your arms at your sides, and your belly button pulled back toward your spine. Elongate your neck and imagine touching the top of your head to the ceiling, but keep your chin parallel to the floor. Rotate your shoulders back and down. Hold and breathe into this position for 30 seconds.

 Modified Tree

Yoga is great way to teach children to balance. This is a common yoga position.

    Tell the children: From a standing position, shift your weight onto your right foot. Raise your left knee and place the bottom of your left foot on your right leg, at the ankle, calf, or knee. Hold your hands out to the sides for balance. Hold this position and count to 10 before returning to the start position. Repeat the movement with other leg.

 Airplane

Challenge the children's balance by asking them to place the body in a different "plane."

    Tell the children: From a standing position, raise your arms out to the side at shoulder level. Balancing on your right leg, swing your left leg behind your body. Bend at the waist. Hold this position and count to 10 before slowly coming back into a standing position. Repeat the movement with the other leg.

 V Sit

Tell the children: Begin by sitting with your legs bent and your feet on the floor. Slowly straighten the right leg so the foot lifts off the floor. You should be balancing on your tailbone. Slowly straighten the left leg, too, so that both feet are off the floor. Your body should now look like the letter V. With your arms, you can grab your legs for support or remain out to the side for balance. Hold for a count of 10, return to the starting position, and repeat 3 times.

33 Isolation Challenges

Tell the children: Stand with your arms straight out to your sides at, shoulder height, with palms down. Keeping your hips still, lift your rib cage and slide it side to side 20 times.

34 Pointer

Tell the children: Begin with hands and knees on the floor. Extend your right leg straight out behind your body, pointing your toes. Hold. Once you feel balanced, begin to move your right leg in a circle, being careful not to move any other part of your body, only your leg. Imagine if your toes are a crayon and you are drawing big circles and little circles. Draw 10 circles. Repeat the movement with the other side of the body 10 times.

35 Twister

Tell the children: In a standing position, stretch your arms out to your sides at shoulder height. Twist your upper body to the left as far as possible; your head and neck should turn with your body. Then twist right. Don't let your arms rotate the body; the torso should be doing the work with the arms just following. Repeat this movement 10 times.

36 Windmill

Tell the children: Begin in a standing position, with your feet farther than hip-distance apart and your arms stretched out to your sides at shoulder height. Twist your torso. Bending and twisting at your waist, bring your right arm to touch your left foot. Come back up to the starting position and repeat the movement on the other side.

Spine Extension

Tell the children: Lie on your stomach with your arms at your sides and place your chin on a mat. Imagine reaching out through the top of your head with a long neck as you lift your head off the floor. Hold the position and breathe before slowly lowering your head. Repeat 5 times.

 Goal Post

Tell the children: Lie facedown. Rest your forehead on a small pillow if needed. Bend your arms to a 90-degree angle and lift them off the floor as high as you can. Holding your arms in the up position, breathe and count to 10 before slowly lowering them again. Repeat 5 times.

 Bicycles

Tell the children: Sit on the floor, with knees bent. Lean back slightly. Bring your right knee toward your chest and extend your left foot out. Switch legs as if cycling.

 Overhead Stretch

Tell the children: Begin in a standing position. Place your left hand on your hip. Straighten your right arm overhead and lean to your left side. Lean and hold the stretch. Change arms. Place right hand on hip. Bring your left arm up overhead and lean to your right side. Hold. Concentrate on stretching and lengthening the body.

 Rock 'n Roll

Props A small pillow for each participant

Tell the children: Lie on your back with your arms by your side and your knees in the air. Place a small pillow between your knees. Roll your knees toward your chest and then bring them back down to starting position. Repeat this movement 10 times.

Hula Hips

Tell the children: Stand with your hands on your waist and your feet wider than hip-distance apart. Circle your hips to the right several times. Reverse, circling your hips to the left several times.

Chop It Off

Tell the children: From a standing position with your arms overhead, squat and rotate your torso quickly by swinging both arms to one side. Your arms will be parallel to the ground as you rotate. Quickly stand up, swinging your arms back overhead, and repeat the exercise on the other side.

Ball Sit

Props A large exercise ball for each participant

Tell the children: Use the largest ball you have. Sit on ball with both feet flat on floor and with your head lifted. Lift one foot off the floor as high as you can, keeping the knee bent, and hold this position for 30 seconds. Slowly lower your foot and repeat with the other side.

Superman on a Ball

Props A large exercise ball for each participant

Tell the children: Place your body facedown over the ball, with your feet touching the floor and your arms overhead. Lift up your right arm with your left leg, hold, and breathe for 15 seconds. Slowly lower that arm and leg and repeat the exercise with your other side.

Pelvic Tilt on a Ball

Props A large exercise ball for each participant

Tell the children: Sit on the center of the ball. Align your knees over your ankles and place your legs hip-width apart. Pull in your belly button, curl your tailbone forward, and let the ball roll slightly forward under your bottom. Push back the tailbone and roll the ball back. Repeat 10 times.

 ## Trunk Twists

Props A small- to medium-size ball for each participant

Tell the children: Sit with your knees bent and together, your feet apart for balance, and a ball between your hands. Lean back at a 45-degree angle—halfway between sitting up straight and lying down. Hold the ball in front of you, arms extended. Looking at the ball, move it from side to side by twisting your upper body 20 times.

 ## Hip Swivels

Props A small- to medium-size ball for each participant

Tell the children: Lie on your back with your knees up and pointing toward the ceiling, arms on the floor extending away from the body. Put a ball between your knees. Slowly rotate your hips from one side to the other, allowing your legs to touch lightly on the floor 20 times.

 ## Tummy Twists

Tell the children: Lie on your back and lift your knees toward your chest. Stretch your arms out at shoulder height on each side of your body. Keeping knees together, slowly lower both knees toward the right side. Do not let your knees touch the ground and do not let your hips come off the ground. Hold in the lowest position. Breathe, count to 5, and slowly return knees to the middle. Now slowly lower both knees toward the left side. Hold, breathe, count to 5, and slowly return to the middle.

50   Seated Knee to Chest

Props A chair for each participant

Tell the children: Sit up straight in a chair, with your feet on the floor. Place your hands on the sides of the chair seat. Slowly raise a knee and bring it as close to your chest as you can, and hold this position for 15 seconds. Be sure you are still sitting up tall in the chair. Slowly return your foot to the floor and repeat 10 times. Then repeat the exercise 10 times with your other leg.

51   T-Shape

Tell the children: Lie facedown with your arms forward, spread open at chest level. Keep your toes, knees, and hips touching the ground. Squeeze your shoulder blades together at your mid-back; raise your arms slightly off the ground. Keep your elbows bent and your palms facing the ground. Hold and breathe for 10 seconds. Release and repeat.

52   Sit-Ups

Divide the group into pairs or have the players choose partners.

    Tell the children: Have your partner sit on the floor with her knees bent and her arms crossed across her chest. Place your hands on her ankles. The sitting partner will lower her upper body to the floor, exhale, and slowly come back up to a seated position. If this is too difficult for either partner, go only halfway down. Each of you should do as many repetitions as you can and then switch roles.

53   Reverse Crunches

Tell the children: Lie on your back and lift your knees toward your chest. Keep your arms flat by your sides. Pull your belly button back toward your spine and roll your hips a couple of inches off the floor. Breathe and repeat 10 times.

54   Double Leg Pull

Tell the children: Lie on your back with your knees bent and your feet flat on the floor. Slide your bottom under so your lower back is pressed against the floor. Raise your shoulders and hug your knees to your chest. Now raise both of your arms overhead while extending your legs straight out and keeping your back flat. Pause and breathe and then return to the starting position. Do as many as you can.

55   Roll Like a Ball

Tell the children: Sit on the floor and hug your knees to your chest. Balance on your tailbone and lift your feet. Pull your stomach muscles in and roll back onto your lower back. Immediately roll back up onto your tailbone and balance. Repeat 10 times.

56   Superman Hold

Divide the group into pairs or have the players choose partners.

    Tell the children: Have your partner lie on the floor facedown. His arms and legs should be stretched out. Grab your partner's ankles and have him slowly lift his upper body off of the floor. Have him hold this position for 3 seconds before lowering to repeat. Each partner should do as many repetitions as they can and then switch roles.

57   Cobra

Tell the children: Lie facedown on the floor with your legs together. Your hands, flat on the floor next to your chest, should be slightly more than shoulder-width apart. Extending your arms, raise your upper body off of the floor. Then, keeping your body straight, lower your body to the floor by bending your arms. Repeat 5 times.

Note Both the upper and lower body must be kept straight throughout this movement.

Developing Muscle Strength

any size

Except as noted

A child's strength-training program shouldn't just be a scaled-down version of an adult's workout program. These exercises are designed to help kids build a sense of balance and control and give them an awareness of their bodies. As with any sport, it's wise to have children visit a doctor before beginning a strength-training regimen. Each of the exercises in this chapter should be learned without resistance. Later, when proper technique is mastered, small amounts of resistance (body weight, band, or other weight) can be added. In general, as kids get older and stronger, they can gradually increase the amount of resistance they use.

58 Beginner Push-Ups

Tell the children: Begin facedown, with your hands and knees on the floor. Place your hands directly beneath your shoulders. Extending your arms and pulling your belly button toward the spine, raise your body. Then, using upper-body strength, slowly lower your body again until your chest almost touches the ground. Do as many push-ups as you can.

59 Wall Push-Ups

Prop A wall

Wall push-ups are a great way to teach anybody how to master a push-up.

Tell the children: Stand about an arm's distance away from a wall with your legs together. Place your hands on the wall just a little farther apart than your shoulders. Lean forward, touch your nose to the wall and then push back to the starting position. Repeat this exercise 20 times, making sure to keep your heels on the floor and your body in a straight line.

 ## Plank Position

Tell the children: Get on your hands and knees, keeping your arms extended straight below your shoulders and your fingers pointing forward. Then straighten your legs behind you and use your back and stomach muscles to lift your stomach off the floor until your whole body forms a straight line from head to toes, making sure not to let your rear end stick up in the air or your back and stomach sag in the middle. Hold this position for 15 seconds.

 ## Biceps Curls

Props A small, spongelike ball or balloon for each participant

Tell the children: In a standing position, with your right arm bent at a 90-degree angle, place a ball or balloon between your biceps and forearm. Close the forearm to keep the ball in place. Squeeze the arm tightly 10 times, rest, and then switch arms.

 ## Stick 'Em Up

Props A chair for each participant

Tell the children: Sit in a chair without your back touching the back of the chair. Pull your belly button toward your spine. Lift your head toward the ceiling, but keep your chin parallel to the ground. Roll your shoulders back and down, keeping them relaxed. Bring your arms up, elbows bent, to shoulder height. Slowly raise your arms up overhead, making sure not to let your shoulders come up. Return your arms to the starting position. Breathe and repeat 10 times.

63 **Bent-Over Lateral Raise**

Props A chair and two small balls for each participant

Tell the children: Hold a ball in each hand. Sit on the edge of a chair with your legs together. Bend forward from your hips so your upper body is parallel to the floor. Pull your belly button back toward your spine. Begin with your arms hanging straight down, palms facing in. Slowly raise the balls to your sides with straight arms until your hands are even with your shoulders. Keep your arms straight, but with your elbows slightly bent and your palms facing down. Squeeze your shoulder blades together as you lift the balls. Hold for 15 seconds, breathe, and then slowly lower your hands to your sides. Repeat this exercise 10 times.

 64 **Triceps Push-Ups**

Props A chair for each participant

Tell the children: Sit on the edge of a chair with your legs hip-distance apart. Place your palms down on the edge of your chair at your sides, with your fingertips curling underneath so they point toward your bottom. Push down with your arms and lift your bottom an inch off the chair, holding the position for 5 seconds. Immediately sit back down again. Repeat this exercise 5 times.

 65 **Overhead Reach**

Tell the children: In a standing position, bring both arms up overhead. Imagine you are climbing up a rope. Leaning slightly to the left, concentrate on stretching and lengthening your body. Lower your right arm until your hand is at shoulder level. Return to a standing position and repeat, leaning to the opposite side.

66   Baseball Swings

Although this is a baseball-related game, no equipment is necessary.

Tell the children: Stand with your feet shoulder-width apart and clasp your hands together in front of your chest. Pull in your belly button, keep your chest high, and extend both of your arms to the right as if you're about to swing a baseball bat. Keeping your shoulders down, slowly bring your arms across your chest as far to the left as possible. Slowly reverse the direction of the movement to return to the starting position. Repeat this movement 10 times. Use muscle control, not speed, to perform this exercise.

67   Wheelbarrow

This is a fun exercise, and kids enjoy being the wheelbarrow. Divide the group into pairs or have the players choose partners.

Tell the children: Have your partner lie facedown on the floor. Stand between his feet, facing his head, and grasp his ankles. Keeping his hands on the floor, he will push up with his arms until they are straight, and you will lift his ankles until you are standing straight and holding his ankles at your sides. Then, with head up, he will walk on his hands forward 20 steps while you walk forward and support his body and he tries not to let it sag. When you are finished, switch roles.

68   Wheelbarrow Push-Ups

Divide the group into pairs or have the players choose partners.

Tell the children: Have your partner lie facedown on the floor. Grasp her ankles and raise her body into a Wheelbarrow position (#67). With her hands on the floor, she will push up with her arms until they are straight. Then, with head up, she will lower her chest back toward the floor to push up again. Try not to let your partner's body sag. After doing this 10 times, switch roles.

69 Stairway Push-Ups

Prop A set of stairs

Standing on the floor, be sure that the children's feet are not slippery or that they are wearing shoes with nonslippery soles.

Tell the children: Start in a standing position in front of the stairs. Then lean forward as if you were falling and place your hands on the same step on which your shoulders would rest if you were to continue falling. Slowly push up and away from the stairs as if doing a push-up. Return to the straight-arm position and repeat the complete movement 20 times.

70 Throwing a Ghost Ball

Tell the children: Pretend to throw a baseball. Go through the entire movement several times with one arm and then switch to the other arm. When you switch, you may find that it feels very different. Repeat the movement several times with each arm.

Variation Have the children pretend to shoot a basketball, going through the same process as with the ghost baseball. Be sure to try this exercise with both arms.

71 Punching Arms

Tell the children: Imagine that a punching bag is hanging in front of you. Using both arms, punch fast, slow, and from different angles. If one hand is leading the punches, switch hands and try this exercise with the other. Repeat several times.

72 Overhead Press

Tell the children: With both elbows bent and both hands in fists and resting just above your shoulders, extend your arms straight up overhead. Return to the starting position and repeat the complete movement 20 times. This exercise can be done with 1–2-pound weights.

73 External Rotation

Tell the children: Lie on your left side on the floor with your legs together and your knees slightly bent. Rest your head in your left hand or lie on your outstretched arm. Position your right arm along your side, bend your elbow at a 90-degree angle, and rest your right forearm on your stomach, with your palm facing your stomach. Keeping your upper arm stationary, slowly raise your right hand as far as you can. Then slowly lower your right hand toward your stomach again. Repeat several times and then switch sides.

74 Triceps Push-Aways

Prop A wall

Tell the children: Stand with your back leaning against a wall and your arms down along your sides, palms touching the wall. Push yourself away from the wall using the palms of your hands. Repeat the motion 10 times.

75 Basketball Hook

Tell the children: Stand tall with your arms at your sides and your feet shoulder-distance apart. Raise your right arm up and out to your side, hand at waist level to start, pulling your belly button back toward your spine as you do. Slightly tilt your body to the left and, in a semicircular motion, extend your right arm back and up toward your shoulder. Reach up and over your head toward the left side as far as you can go. Perform this movement very slowly. Repeat 10 times and then switch sides.

76 Boxing

Tell the children: Stand with your feet shoulder-width apart. Bend your arms at the elbows, bringing them toward your body and keeping your fists at chin level. Moving from the waist and not the knees, slowly bend your upper body down and to the left, as if avoiding a punch thrown at your head. Return to the center and alternate side to side 20 times.

77 Speed Bag

Tell the children: In a standing position, bring both arms up to chest height in front of you. Bending at the elbows, bring your fists together, one on top of the other. Imagine a speed bag in front of your chin and begin rotating fist over fist as fast as you can, repeating the movement for 30 seconds before reversing the rotation. Be careful not to punch yourself.

78 Towel Tug of War

Props Two bath towels for each pair

Divide the group into pairs or have the players choose partners.

   Tell the children: Stand facing your partner. Take two bath towels and loop them together, so that each person has two ends to grip in his hands. As your partner begins to pull the towels toward his chest, challenge his strength by adding some resistance. Repeat this exercise 20 times and then switch roles.

79 Towel Pull-Downs

Props A bath towel for each pair

Divide the group into pairs or have the players choose partners.

   Tell the children: One partner kneels on the floor and takes hold of one end (two corners) of a towel. Meanwhile, the other partner stands above, holding the other end of the towel. The object of this movement is for the kneeling partner to pull down on the towel while her standing partner challenges her strength by adding resistance. Repeat this exercise 25 times.

80 Chest Squeeze

Props A small- to medium-size firm ball for each participant

Tell the children: In a standing position, take hold of a ball between the palms of your hands. Holding the ball at chest height, press your hands firmly into the ball. Bring your arms up overhead while squeezing the ball and then lower them. Repeat this exercise 30 times.

81   Lateral Lift, Palms Down

Divide the group into pairs or have the players choose partners.

Tell the children: Stand facing your partner. Have your partner raise his arms out to his sides at shoulder height, palms down. Place your hands lightly on top of his hands. Have your partner slowly lift his arms up, while you apply light resistance. Hold the press, rest, and repeat 25 times before switching roles.

82   Lateral Lift, Palms Up

Divide the group into pairs or have the players choose partners.

Tell the children: Stand facing your partner. Have your partner raise her arms out to her sides at shoulder height, palms up. Place your hands lightly on top of her hands. Have your partner slowly lift her arms up, while you apply light resistance. Hold the press, rest, and repeat 25 times before switching roles.

83   Frontal Lift, Palms Down

Divide the group into pairs or have the players choose partners.

Tell the children: Stand facing your partner. Have your partner raise her arms straight out in front at shoulder height, palms down, Place your hands lightly on top of her hands. Have your partner slowly lift her arms up while you apply light resistance. Hold the press, rest and repeat 25 times before switching roles.

84 Frontal Lift, Palms Up

Divide the group into pairs or have the players choose partners.

Tell the children: Stand facing your partner. Have your partner raise his arms straight out in front at shoulder height, palms up. Place your hands lightly on top of his hands. Have your partner slowly lift his arms up while you apply light resistance. Hold the press, rest, and repeat 25 times before switching roles.

85 Biceps Resistance

Divide the group into pairs or have the players choose partners.

Tell the children: Stand behind your partner. Have her make fists, with her hands turned palm up. Next, asking her to keep her elbows at her sides, have your partner bend her arms at the elbow. Place your hands on top of her fists. Instruct her to bring her fists toward her shoulders while you apply gentle pressure. Repeat 25 times and then switch roles.

Variation If one partner isn't quite tall enough to stand behind the other and perform this exercise, he may stand in front of her.

86 Reverse-Fly Resistance

Divide the group into pairs or have the players choose partners.

Tell the children: Stand facing your partner. To begin, place your arms straight down in front of your body, shoulder-width apart, with your palms facing each other. Your partner then places his arms inside of your arms by your wrists. The object is to have your partner push your arms open while you provide resistance. Repeat this exercise 10 times and then switch roles.

Note If one partner is taller than the other, have the tall partner sit in a chair.

Variation If the partners are strong, they can perform this exercise one arm at a time.

Outdoor Playground

The time spent together with your kids at a playground may be one of the biggest benefits of a playground workout, but the equipment definitely still provides exercise. Climbing on the monkey bars challenges a child's upper body as she holds on to each bar, feet off the ground, and moves from one bar to the next, using only her hands. The teeter-totter provides an excellent opportunity to strengthen legs, as she pushes up and then softly lands using only her legs. And pumping the swing higher and higher is a good workout for both leg and the stomach muscles—for kids and adults.

The following workouts include exercises for the buttocks, hips, thighs, and legs.

88

The Plié

Tell the children: Stand with your heels together and then turn your toes out as far as you can. The goal is to turn your toes away from each other, as if to form a straight line. Slowly bend your knees to the sides, dropping your bottom toward the floor. Hold in this down position before slowly coming back to a standing position. Repeat this movement 20 times.

89

Squats

Tell the children: Stand with your feet hip-width apart, toes pointing forward. Bend your knees as if you were going to sit back in a chair, slowly counting, "1, 2, 3, 4" until your thighs are as close to parallel to the floor as possible. Hold this pose for two seconds and then straighten your legs to the starting position. Repeat this exercise 20 times.

90   The Elevé

Tell the children: In a standing position, hold onto a steady surface. Then, starting with your feet in a turned-out position, rise to the balls of your feet. Lower back into the starting position. Perform as many of these as you can.

91   The Rond de Jambe

Tell the children: Stand with your weight on your right leg. Lift your left foot slightly and, with toes pointed and still touching the floor, circle your foot slowly from the front of your body to the back, skimming the floor with your toe. Return the foot to the starting position and then repeat the complete movement 10 times before switching to your other leg.

92   Lunge

Tell the children: In a standing position with your hands on your hips and your feet shoulder-width apart, take a large step forward with your right leg. Slowly bend your knees until your right thigh is parallel to the floor. Both knees should be bent at a 90-degree angle and the right knee should not pass the tips of your toes. Slowly lift your body and step back into the starting position, pushing through the heel of your right foot. Repeat this movement with the same leg 30 times and then switch legs.

93   Walking Lunge

Tell the children: In a standing position with your hands on yours hips and your feet shoulder-width apart, take a large step forward with your right leg. Slowly bend your knees until your right thigh is parallel to the floor. Both knees should be bent at a 90-degree angle, and the right knee should not pass the tips of your toes. Slowly lift your body and step forward with your left leg into a lunge. Repeat this movement 30 times.

94 Squat Walk

Tell the children: Stand with your feet hip-width apart and your toes pointing forward. Bend your knees as if you were going to sit back in a chair, slowly counting, "1, 2, 3, 4" until your thighs are as close to parallel to the floor as possible. Hold this position as you walk forward 4 steps and then backward 4 steps to where you started. Repeat the whole series of movements 10 times.

95 Sit Kicks

Tell the children: Sit on the floor, with your knees bent and your feet flat. Place your hands palms down on the floor behind you. Lean back slightly and extend your right leg off the floor into a kick. Kick 30 times with this leg before switching legs.

Variation This exercise can be done alternating the leg that kicks, too.

96 Temper Tantrum

Tell the children: Lie facedown on the floor with your arms outstretched past your head and your legs extended long. Quickly begin to alternate kicks, bringing your heels toward your bottom. Do this exercise repeatedly for 1 minute.

97 Scuttle Bug

Tell the children: Begin in a crawl position with your hands and feet on the floor and your bottom pointing toward the ceiling. Crawl several steps forward, backward, and sideways. This is a great exercise for your upper body, too. Do this exercise repeatedly for 1 minute.

98   Inner-Thigh Lifts

Tell the children: Lie on your right side with your right leg straight. Bend your left knee and place your left foot on the floor behind your right knee. Rest your head in your right hand or on your outstretched right arm. Keeping your right leg straight and your toes pulled in, slowly raise your leg up toward your left knee. Pull your belly button back toward your spine. Hold your leg in the up position before slowly lowering it to the floor. Repeat this movement 20 times and then switch legs.

99   Imaginary Bicycle

Tell the children: Lie on your back with your feet up in the air. Pedal your feet as if you were pedaling a bicycle. Pedal fast, slow, backward, and wide-legged for 1 minute.

100   Bridge

Tell the children: Lie on your back with your knees bent and the bottoms of your feet flat on the floor. Lift your hips off the floor as high as possible and count to 10. Then slowly lower your body back to the starting position. Repeat the exercise 5 times.

101   Bottom Walking

Tell the children: Sit on the floor with your legs outstretched in front of you. Lift your right hip up and forward and then your left hip up and forward so that you are "walking" forward. Walk forward 10 times and then backward 10 times.

Variation Have the children Bottom Walk with their hands on their hips and with their arms outstretched to the sides to see how each affects their movement.

102 Crab Walk

This exercise is good for all kids—and parents, too.

Tell the children: Sit on the floor with your knees bent, your feet flat on floor, and your hands flat and behind your body. Lift your hips off the floor, supporting yourself on your feet and hands. Walk backward and forward for 1 minute.

103 Crab Kicks

Tell the children: Start in the Crab Walk position (#102), with your bottom up off the floor and your knees at right angles to it. Kick up your right leg and then your left leg. Count how many kicks you can do in 1 minute.

104 Heel to Bottom

Props A counter top or a chair for each participant

Tell the children: Stand, holding on to a kitchen counter or a chair for balance for this exercise. Bending your right leg, bring your right heel toward your bottom. Try this 30 times and then switch legs.

105 Kneeling Kickbacks

Tell the children: Kneel on all fours. Keeping your right knee bent at a 90-degree angle, slowly lift your right leg until your thigh is parallel to the floor. Pause for a moment and then slowly lower your leg back to the floor. Repeat this movement 10 times and then switch legs.

Towel Slide

Props A towel for each participant

Note This exercise works best on hardwood floors or other slippery surfaces.

Tell the children: Stand with a towel under your left foot. Lean back slightly, bending your right knee, and slide your left leg out to the side, keeping that knee straight. Slide your leg back to the center and then return to the standing position. Repeat 10 times and then switch sides.

 Step Dip

Prop A step

Tell the children: Sit on a bottom step, feet on the floor, and grasp the front edge of the step with both hands. Now slide your bottom off the step while walking your feet forward a little but keep your hands in place on the step. Slowly bend your elbows and lower your hips until your shoulders are in line with your elbows. Push back up to start again. See if you can do 10 Step Dips.

 Wall Sitting

Prop A wall

Tell the children: Stand with your back to the wall and your feet parallel to each other. Keep your back straight against the wall. Bend your knees to slide slowly down the wall. Your lower legs should remain parallel to the wall. Hold this position as long as you can and then slide back up the wall. Repeat 5 times.

109 Sofa Lifts

Prop A sofa

Tell the children: Lie on your back on the floor with your heels and ankles on the edge of the sofa. Bend your knees slightly and have your arms at your sides. Press your left heel into the sofa and bend your right knee in toward your chest. Lift your torso off of the floor. Hold this position for 5 seconds and then lower your torso to the floor. Begin again, with legs switching roles. Repeat the entire sequence 10 times.

110 Kneeling Side Kicks

Tell the children: Begin on all fours. Balance on your right knee and both hands. Lift your left knee up off the floor and out to the side. Hold your left knee at hip height. Extend and bend your left leg 10 times. Return to the starting position and then switch sides.

111 Leg Circles

Tell the children: Lie on your back on the floor with your knees bent and your arms outstretched to your sides. Extend your right leg into the air and slowly draw an imaginary circle with that foot. Keep your torso as still as possible. Repeat 30 times and then lower your leg. Switch legs to draw a circle with your other foot.

112 Supine Leg Slide

Props Two towels for each participant

Note This exercise works best on hardwood floors or other slippery surfaces.

Tell the children: Lie on your back with your knees bent and a towel under each foot. Lift your hips slightly off the floor, press into your left heel, slide that foot, and straighten the leg. Now bend your left knee and slide that leg back in as you slide your right leg out, keeping hips lifted. Repeat 10 times per leg.

113 Reverse Froggie

Tell the children: Lie facedown on the floor with your heels together. Your knees should be bent and turned out. Pull your belly button in, draw your tailbone down, and rest your forehead on your hands. Keeping heels together, contract your bottom muscles to lift your thighs off the ground. Hold in the up position for 15 seconds and then release. Repeat 5 times.

114 Stair Climbing

Prop A set of stairs

Find a long set of steps. It is better if the stairs are outside.

    Tell the children: Run up the steps but walk back down the steps. (It's better for your knees.) Repeat this for 5 minutes.

115 Resistant Leg Lifts

Props A chair for each pair

Divide the group into pairs or have the players choose partners.

    Tell the children: Have your partner sit tall in a chair, bending his legs at the knees. Place your hand gently on the top of his thigh just above the knee. As he slowly brings his knee up, gently press his thigh down. Hold the resistance for 15 seconds and repeat the lift 5 times before switching legs. Then switch roles.

116 Hamstring Curls with Resistance

Divide the group into pairs or have the players choose partners.

Tell the children: Have your partner lie facedown on the floor, arms down at her sides. Have her bend at the knee, one leg at a time, bringing her heel toward her bottom. Place your hand at her ankle and provide light resistance as she brings her leg up. Repeat 10 times before switching legs. Then switch roles.

117 Bridge Partner

Divide the group into pairs or have the players choose partners.

Tell the children: Your partner begins on all fours. You lie on your back on the floor, placing the heels of your feet on top of your partner's back, with your toes pointing toward the ceiling. Pull your belly button toward your spine and flatten your lower back into the floor. Keep your arms outstretched to your sides on the floor. Press your hips up off the floor and squeeze your bottom, while pressing the heels of your feet into your partner's back. Press upward until your legs and hips are in line with your torso. Hold for 15 seconds and then slowly release lowering your body to the starting position. Repeat a 10 times and then switch roles.

Note If one partner is taller than the other—particularly if one partner is an adult—that partner may have to drop onto her elbows so the shorter partner can place the heels of his feet on the other's back.

Cardiovascular Exercises

Except
as noted

Cardiovascular exercise challenges and strengthens your cardiovascular system, which includes your heart, blood, and the blood vessels that carry blood to and from your heart.

Dance

Tell the children: Any physical movement is exercise, so use your imagination. If you love to dance, put on your favorite music and dance for 10 minutes. Keep it fun.

119 Running in Place

Tell the children: Run in place for 1 minute, trying as many different running styles as you can imagine: high knees, heels kicking your bottom, wide-leg running, or slow-motion running. If the weather permits, do this exercise outside.

Jump Rope, Both Feet Low

Props A jump rope for each participant

Tell the children: Swing the rope smoothly and keep your feet close to the ground. Hold your elbows at your sides, turning the rope with your wrists. As the rope circles toward your feet, jump it. Count how many jumps you can do without stopping.

121   Jump Rope, Both Feet High

Props A jump rope for each participant

Tell the children: As the rope circles toward your feet, jump it, bringing both feet up high. Do this for 1 minute.

122   Jump Rope, One Foot Only

Props A jump rope for each participant

Tell the children: As the rope circles toward your feet, jump over the rope using only one foot the entire time. Do this for 1 minute.

123   Jump Rope, Alternating Feet

Props A jump rope for each participant

Tell the children: As the rope circles toward your feet, jump over the rope, alternating the leg that is leading, for 1 minute.

124   Scissor Jumps

Tell the children: Begin in a standing position with one foot in front of the other. Jump up and switch the locations of your front foot and your back foot. Try this exercise slowly and then speed up the movement. Repeat this movement 20 times.

Jump Rope, Scissor Jumps

Props A jump rope for each participant

Tell the children: As the rope circles toward your feet, jump over it first with your right leg in front and your left leg in the back; when the rope comes around again, switch the leg that leads, and keep alternating the leading leg in this way. Do this for 1 minute.

 ## Jumping Jacks

Tell the children: Jump and land with your feet wide apart; jump and land with your feet together. Each set of one wide and one feet-together jump counts as one Jumping Jack. Do 15 Jumping Jacks.

Variation To make this more challenging, add an arm movement. To do this, when your legs are together, your straightened arms are down at the sides of your legs. As you jump wide, raise your straightened arms sideways and upward until they are overhead.

Note Learning the coordination to use their arms and legs together may take awhile for some children.

 ## Skipping

Skipping is one of those exercises that all children should learn. It helps with coordination, rhythm, and timing.

Practice skipping yourself and then demonstrate the movement to the children. Sometimes children have a hard time learning to skip, but it's an important skill to learn.

Tell the children: Step forward with your right foot, and then bring your left knee up and scoot forward at the same time. Immediately step forward with left foot and raise your right knee into a knee-lift-scoot. Repeat this series of movements 30 times.

Note To help the kids remember what to do, say, "Step, knee lift, scoot forward" as they do the exercise.

128 Donkey Kicks

Tell the children: Keeping your feet on the floor, bend over at the waist until you can place the palms of your hands on the floor. "Walk" your hands slightly forward, and allow your buttocks to point up toward the ceiling. Swing your right leg up into a kick toward the ceiling. Try this 5 times with one leg and then switch to the other leg and repeat 5 times.

129 High Kicks

Tell the children: In a standing position, swing your right leg and kick it up as high as you can in front of your body. Repeat this movement 5 times and then switch legs, repeating 5 times with your left leg. Be careful not to use your back when kicking.

130 Frog Jump

Tell the children: Just like a frog, get into a squat position with your hands and feet on the floor. Jump up as high and as far forward as you can. Repeat this movement 20 times.

131 Knee Taps

Tell the children: Run in place, bringing your knees up in front of your body. Using both hands, try to tap the knee that is in the up position. Repeat this movement 30 times.

132 Squats with Diagonal Jump-Ups

Tell the children: Stand with your feet hip-width apart and extend your arms in front of your chest. Squat and then rotate the torso to the left as if you are going to touch the front of your left foot. Jump up, rotate your torso to the right, and extend your arms over your right shoulder. Return to the starting position and repeat the squat. This time, reach down for the right foot and then jump up, extending your arms over your left shoulder. Continue to alternate sides, repeating the movement 20 times.

133 Side Lateral Leaps

Tell the children: Stand with your feet together and your weight on the right foot. Bend your knees and leap off your right foot, moving to the left as far as you can. Keep your knees in line with your feet. Land softly, with your feet together and your elbows bent at your sides. Return to the starting position, and this time put your weight on your left foot, bend your knees, and push off to your right side. Repeat this movement 10 times on each side.

134 Push-Backs

Tell the children: Stand with your feet slightly apart and your hands on your hips. Placing your weight on your right foot, extend your left leg behind you until only your toes touch the floor, creating a straight line from left heel to hips. Keeping your weight balanced over your right foot and your hips level, lean forward from your hips until your upper body and left leg are parallel to the floor. Hold this position for 10 seconds and then lower yourself back into the starting position. Repeat with your other leg. Repeat this exercise 20 times.

135 Elbow–Knee

Tell the children: Stand with your feet a few inches apart. Bend your arms at the elbows; bring them up and out to the sides so that you look like a goalpost. Jump up and bring your left knee up toward your right elbow, twisting your torso to help you reach. Then return your leg to the starting position and repeat the movement, but this time bring your right knee up to your left side. Repeat this movement 20 times.

136 Tuck Jumps

Tell the children: Start in a standing position. Bend your knees. Then jump up, bringing your knees up in front of your body and slapping your hands onto them. Repeat the movement 15 times.

Speed Skate

Tell the children: Stand with your feet together, arms at your sides. Jump to the right, leading with your right leg. Your left leg then follows and crosses behind your right foot as you land. Simultaneously, reach your left arm across your body as if you're trying to touch the floor. Repeat the motion, jumping to the left. Jump side to side as quickly as possible 30 times.

Side Skip-Ups

Tell the children: Begin in a standing position. Bend your knees and shift your body weight to the ball of your left foot. Then skip up, pushing with your left foot, jumping straight up, and bending your right knee at the top of the jump. Return to the starting position and skip up again, this time pushing off your right leg, jumping straight up, and bending your left knee at the top of the jump. Repeat this sequence for 1 minute.

Plank Jumps

Tell the children: In a Squat position (#89) with your hands touching the ground in front of your knees (same position as if you are doing a Forward Roll [#233]), shift your weight to your hands and jump both feet back into a Plank Position (#60). Immediately jump feet back into the starting position. Repeat this series of movements 10 times.

Biking

Props A bicycle and bike helmet for each participant

Riding a bike is a great cardiovascular exercise. Go biking for 30 minutes.

141 Hiking

Let the world be your gym. Explore the great outdoors by hiking trails, or walking through the woods and fields. Try hiking for 60 minutes.

Variations Try geocaching or orienteering.

Geocaching

Search for treasure! Go to www.geocaching
.com and search for geocaching in your local
area. If you don't have a geocaching organi-
zation in your area, start one in your local
park. Geocaching is a GPS-powered treasure hunt, and, according to a new study,
it may hold the key to getting kids and
family members to exercise.

Orienteering

Orienteering is a fun form of land
navigation for the entire family.
This sport started out as a form of
military training in the nineteenth
century and has become a popular
sport for everyone. You will need a com-
pass and a detailed map to find points in the landscape. Orienteering can be
enjoyed as a walk in the woods to learn to use a compass or it can be done as a
professional sport, in which it is a timed event.

A standard orienteering course consists of a start and a series of points,
called control sites or clues, which are designated on the map. By following
the symbols on the map, you try to find each clue. When you find the clue, you
verify your visit by using a paper-hole punch hanging next to the flag to mark
your control card. Follow all the clues and head for the finish line. Many different types of orienteering exist, such as foot, mountain bike, skiing, trail,
and canoe orienteering. You can make up your own orienteering game by
planning a route on a map and then timing the route. It's a great way to learn,
enjoy nature, burn calories, and enjoy your family and friends.

Swimming

Prop A pool

Swimming offers exercises for all ages and skill levels to do in the water. Swim
laps, play games, or, for additional fitness ideas, check out *101 Cool Pool Games
for Children* (Hunter House Publishers).

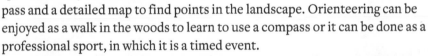

Thirty Movement Patterns

Following specific movement patterns challenges coordination skills and provides cardiovascular exercise.

143 Toe–Heel Kicks

Tell the children: Stand with your feet shoulder-width apart and your left foot slightly in front of your right foot. Bring your arms in front of your chest in a boxing stance.

Begin by alternately tapping the toes of your front and rear foot for 30 seconds. While keeping this rocking motion going, kick your left heel forward, lean forward until your upper body is almost parallel to the floor, and kick your right heel back. Repeat this movement several times, jog in place for 30 seconds, and then repeat the entire combination 10 times.

144 Punches with Knee Lift

Tell the children: Stand with your feet wide apart. Twist from the waist and punch out to the right with your left arm 3 times. Then lift your left knee and bring your left elbow to meet it. The series is punch, punch, punch, knee lift. Repeat this combination 10 times before switching sides and punching with the other arm.

145 Leap with High Knees

Tell the children: Leap forward 4 times on a diagonal. Keep your knees soft when you are landing. Run backward, bringing your knees up high in front of your body, for 8 steps. Repeat this combination 4 times.

146 Cross Passé with Scissor Jumps

Tell the children: Stand with your feet shoulder-width apart and your arms overhead. Lift your left knee out to the side as you bring your left elbow down to meet it. Hop on your right foot each time you bring the left knee to your elbow. Do this 10 times and then do 10 Scissor Jumps (#124). Return to the starting position and repeat the combination, leading with the other leg.

147 Jump-Up and Jump Switch

Tell the children: In a standing position, jump up as high as you can with your arms overhead. Then, immediately jump down—palms on the floor—with your left foot between your hands and your right leg extended behind you. Lift your hips, jump, and switch legs; repeat this combination 10 times. Then immediately jump back up into the air with your arms overhead.

148 Squat Walk Sideways, Leg-Lift Lunge

Tell the children: From a standing position with hands on hips, Squat Walk (#94) to your left 2 times, taking wide steps. Stop. Shift your weight to your left foot, lunge to your right side, bring your right leg up for a side lift, and then move it back into a lunge position. Return to a standing position and then repeat the sequence starting in the opposite direction. Repeat this combination 5 times.

149 Flipping the Table

Tell the children: Start in a Plank Position (#60), balancing on your hands and toes. Do 1 Push-Up (#58) and then slowly turn your body to the left, lifting your left hand off the ground. Flip over onto your back and look at the ceiling, with your feet flat on the floor, your toes pointing away from your body, your hands under your shoulders, and your body off the floor, forming a straight line from your head to your feet. Lower your bottom to the floor and press your hips back up for 1 Bridge (#100). Roll back over into a Plank Position (#60) and repeat the combination 5 times.

Note If a regular Push-Up position is too difficult for some participants, tell them that they can do Push-Ups on their knees instead.

150 Lunge, Jump-Up with Skipping

Tell the children: Stand with your feet hip-width apart. Push off your left foot, step sideways into a Lunge (#92), and then jump up and onto your left foot for a side Lunge. Alternate Lunging and jumping 6 times, Skip forward (#127) with high knees 4 times, and Skip backward 4 times. Return to the starting position and repeat the entire combination 5 times.

151 Squat Low, Jump High with Basketball

Props A basketball for each participant

Tell the children: Hold a basketball in your hands. Squat low, dribbling the ball to the ground, and then explode upward, bringing the basketball overhead. Repeat this 10 times.

152 Single-Leg Stretch, Single-Knee Chest

Tell the children: Lie on your back with your legs extended. Bring your left knee in toward your chest and, at the same time, lift your right leg off the floor. Alternate knees into chest, keeping your feet off the floor. Do this 10 times. Roll over and get onto your hands and knees. Bring your right knee into your chest and return it to the ground. Then bring your left knee toward your chest and return it to the ground. Do this 10 times before rolling over and returning to the starting position. Repeat the entire combination 5 times.

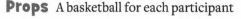

153 Squats/Walking Lunges

Tell the children: Stand with your feet hip-width apart, your knees slightly bent, and your hands on your hips. Squat (#89) 4 times, stand up, and Walking Lunge (#92) 4 times. Repeat the entire combination 5 times.

154 Chicago Squat Walk

Tell the children: Squat Walk (#94) forward 8 steps, run diagonally forward 8 steps, jump up 8 times, and run backward 8 steps. Repeat the entire combination 5 times.

155 Jack Travel

Tell the children: Do 8 Scissor Jumps (#124), do 8 Jumping Jacks (#126) traveling backward, and do 8 Lunges (#92). Repeat the entire combination 5 times.

156 Knee-Ups

Tell the children: From a standing position, lift your left knee to the opposite elbow and then return to the starting position. Then switch legs and arms. Do this 8 times, moving forward. Then do 8 Scissor Jumps (#124). Repeat the entire combination 5 times.

157 Circle Cardio

Tell the children: Run in a large circle for 16 steps, stop using front kicks, travel forward 8 steps. Then do 8 hops backward and run in a circle for 16 steps. Repeat the entire combination 5 times.

158   Cardio Ball

Props   A large exercise ball for each participant

Tell the children: Roll Like a Ball (#55) 4 times, Ball Sit (#44) 4 times, and finish with 4 Basketball Hook (#75) stretches. Repeat the entire sequence 5 times.

159   Motion Combination

Tell the children: Run forward for 16 steps and then leap backward for 16 steps. Repeat the entire combination 5 times.

160   Quadriceps Challenge

Tell the children: Frog Jump (#130) forward 8 times, Squat (#89) 8 times, roll backward 8 times, and finish with another 8 squats. Repeat the entire combination 5 times.

161   Box Step

Tell the children: This is a variation of the traditional box step. Shuffle to your right side 8 steps, run forward 8 steps, shuffle to your left side 8 steps, and run backward 8 steps. Repeat the entire combination 5 times.

162   New York, New York

Tell the children: Do 8 High Kicks (#129) with alternating legs while traveling forward, do 16 Jump-Ups (#228), and then turn around and do 8 more High Kicks with alternating legs while traveling forward. Repeat the entire combination 5 times.

163   Ski Prep

Tell the children: Do 16 Scissor Jumps (#124), 16 Jumping Jacks (#126), 16 Jump-Ups (#228), and 16 High Kicks (#129). Repeat entire sequence 5 times.

164 Face of a Clock

Tell the children: Imagine you are standing in the middle of the face of a clock. Now run forward to 12 o'clock in 4 steps, run backward 4 steps, now run forward to 1 o'clock...and so on through each number on the clock face. Repeat this one time in a clockwise direction.

Variations

- Once the children have participated in the game above, challenge their coordination skills by calling out the numbers in a counter-clockwise direction.

- In a group of three or more players, have one child call out the directions while the others run.

165 Stale Fish

Tell the children: Do 8 Lunges (#92) traveling forward, 8 Lunges traveling backward, and 16 in-place side-to-side lunges. Repeat the entire combination 5 times.

166 Hot Dog

Tell the children: Do 8 hops forward, 8 hops backward, 8 Jump-Ups (#228), and 8 Jumping Jacks (#126). Repeat the entire combination 5 times.

167 Caboose

Tell the children: Run forward 8 steps, jump forward and then backward 8 times, High Kick (#129) 8 times traveling backward, Squat Walk (#94) 8 steps. Repeat the entire combination 5 times.

168 Slide Combination

Tell the children: Shuffle to your right side 8 steps and do 8 Push-Ups (#58) and 8 Jumping Jacks (#126). Slide to your left 8 steps and do 8 Push-Ups and 8 Jumping Jacks. Repeat the entire combination 5 times.

169 Killer Legs

Tell the children: Squat Walk (#94) sideways to your right 8 times, Jump-Up (#228) 8 times, High Kick (#129) 8 times, and then Squat Walk sideways to your left 8 times. Repeat the entire combination 5 times.

170 The Gym

Tell the children: Do Tuck Jumps (#136) for 2 minutes and then do 8 High Kicks (#129), 8 Punches (#71), and 8 more High Kicks. Repeat the entire combination 5 times.

171 Imaginary Force

Tell the children: Do the Imaginary Bicycle (#99) for 1 minute and then jump an imaginary jump rope for 1 minute. Repeat the entire sequence 5 times.

172 Aerobics-Class Combination

Tell the children: March forward 4 steps. Then do 8 Jumping Jacks (#126), 8 High Kicks (#129) alternating legs and traveling backward, and 8 Speed Skates (#137). Repeat the entire combination 5 times.

Fitness Games

Except
as noted

Fitness games involve more than running around. These games promote personal wellness and self-esteem through teamwork and strategies. The following games are challenging and enjoyable to all kids and are not designed to show weakness in kids. Group activities need to encourage problem solving and social interaction between kids.

Sports Training and Coordination Skills

Motor development progresses through a sequence of skill levels. It is important to teach children the fundamentals of physical skills before they move on to more complex skills. To develop endurance, strength, balance, and flexibility, children need exercises that help them develop a variety of different movement skills. These fine and gross motor skills help develop dexterity, muscle strength, hand–eye coordination, and sensory perception. Developing fine motor skills is the building block for developing the larger motor skills, such as shooting a basketball into a hoop.

**Demonstrate an exercise first.
Then teach the children how to perform it.**

Balance is the foundation of every physical skill.

 Balance a Book

Props A book for each participant

Tell the children: Stand with your feet hip-distance apart, arms at your sides, and belly button pulled back toward your spine. Elongate your neck but keep your chin parallel to the floor. Balance a book on your head and begin to walk slowly. Take 10 steps, turn around, and walk back 10 steps. Repeat this exercise 5 times.

174 Close Your Eyes

This level will challenge your child one step further by having them close their eyes.

Tell the children: Stand perfectly straight with your arms down by your sides and your eyes closed. Now bring one foot off of the floor and hold this position for 10 seconds. Do this 5 times and then repeat the exercise 5 times with your other leg.

175 Heel Up

Props A chair for each participant

Tell the children: From a standing position, shift your weight to your right foot. You may need to hold on to something, such as a chair or someone's hand. Bend your left knee and bring your left heel up behind you. Without using your hands, hold your foot as close to your bottom as you can get it. Remain in this position for a count of 10. Return your left foot to the mat. Repeat this exercise 10 times with this leg and then repeat the exercise 10 times using your other leg.

Variation Challenge children who are comfortable in this position by asking them to grab the raised ankle with their hands and pull the heel closer to the buttocks.

176 Put On Your Shoe!

Props A pair of each participant's shoes

Tell the children: Sometimes falling out of balance can help you improve your balance by strengthening the supporting muscles. In a standing position, try putting on your shoes, one shoe at a time. Repeat this 10 times and then switch to the other leg.

Variation If this movement is easy for some children, have them try tying their shoes, too.

177 Walk the Line

Props Tape, chalk, or a rope

To help with dynamic balance, have the children make and walk a straight line. This simple exercise really does improve balance.

Tell the children: Make a straight line using a length of tape on the floor, sidewalk chalk on the playground, or the edge of a curb. Walk the line placing your feet heel to toe.

Tip Tell the participants to keep their eyes on the end of the rope, line, or tape. This will make walking and keeping their balance a little easier.

178 Balance and Catch

Props A ball for each pair

This game will challenge balance, hand–eye coordination, and timing. Divide the group into pairs or have the players choose partners.

Tell the children: Have your partner stand off to one side. You will toss the ball to her while she is trying to complete one of the following four balance challenges:

1. Have your partner walk a straight line. As she does, toss the ball to her. She must immediately throw the ball back to you. Do this 10 times.

2. Have your partner walk backward on the straight line. She must catch and throw back the ball you toss to her. Do this 10 times.

3. Standing on one leg, your partner catches the ball you toss and throws it back to you. Do this 10 times.

4. Standing on one leg, your partner jumps up and down. She must catch the ball you toss to her and throw it back. Do this 10 times.

179 Balance Challenge

Tell the children: Stand on one leg, close your eyes, and count how long you can keep your balance. Repeat this 10 times and then switch to the other leg.

Variations To make this more challenging, stand on one leg and try these variations:

- Place both arms overhead.
- Raise one hand while keeping the other hand down.
- Perform arm circles with both arms.
- Close your eyes and try to touch your nose.

Repeat the variation 10 times and then switch to the other leg.

180 Knee-Up and Extend

Tell the children: Stand with your hands on your hips; shift your weight to the right foot. Lift your left foot slightly so just the ball of the foot is touching the ground. Lift your left knee up so that the foot leaves the ground. Then bring your leg down and extend it out to the side without letting the foot touch the ground. Return to the starting position. Repeat the movement 10 times and then switch to the other leg.

181 Step-Ups

Props A step for each participant

Tell the children: Stand facing a step. Step up onto it with one foot, leaving the other foot behind so that it is not touching the step. Repeat this movement 10 times and then switch to the other leg.

182 Balancing Kicks

Tell the children: This exercise is meant to be performed at a slow pace. Begin in a standing position. Keeping your arms out to your sides to help you maintain balance, shift your weight to stand on one leg. Bend your other leg at the knee, bringing your foot up under you until your heel is touching your bottom. Then kick straight out in front of your body. Bring your heel back under your bottom and step back down into the starting position. Repeat this exercise 5 times, then switch legs and do the exercise 5 more times.

Leg Stands

Tell the children: Start out standing on one leg. Bending at the waist, try to keep your balance as you pick up an object off the ground. Repeat this exercise 10 times.

Variations

- Stand on one foot. Move your arms in different positions: overhead, one up and one down, at shoulder height, one forward and one back.
- Stand on one leg and close your eyes.

Figure-4 Lunges

Tell the children: Standing on your left leg with your hands on your hips, bend your right knee and place the toes of your right foot behind your left calf, Turn your right knee out, bend your left knee, and step back to the right on a diagonal with your right foot flat and your toes turned out. Push off with your right foot and straighten your left leg to return to the starting position. Repeat this set of movements 10 times before switching to the other leg.

Falling Paper

Props A small to large sheet of paper for each pair

Divide the group into pairs or have the players choose partners.

Tell the children: Begin in a standing position with your partner sitting across from you on the floor. Hold a sheet of paper overhead and drop it in front of him. Your partner must try to catch the falling paper using only his fingertips. After doing this for 3 minutes, switch roles.

186 Got It

Props A variety of soft objects of different sizes and shapes for each pair

Divide the group into pairs or have the players choose partners.

Tell the children: Your partner lies face up on the floor, resting on her elbows with her legs about 8 to 10 inches off the floor. You stand above her feet, facing her. Drop one item at a time. The object of this exercise is for the partner on the floor to catch the falling objects with her feet while keeping her feet off the floor. Do this 10 times and then switch roles.

187 The Picker Upper

Props A soft ball or pillow for each participant

Tell the children: Begin sitting on the floor. Then, with a pillow or a soft ball and using only the inside of your ankles, grab the soft object, squeeze and lift it off the floor, and then set it back down. Repeat this exercise 10 times.

188 Toe Gripping

Props Small objects, such as marbles; a bucket for each participant

Tell the children: Using only your toes, pick up small objects (marbles, small plastic toys, etc.) from the floor and place them in a bucket. When the last object is dropped into the bucket, knock it over and start again. Do this 10 times.

By the time a child reaches the ages of 6 to 8, her eyes have usually achieved their normal round shape, and the muscles of the eye can now help track and follow moving objects.

189   Juggling

Props   A ball for each participant

Demonstrate this movement for the children
first. Juggling requires top skills in hand–
eye coordination and timing. To teach the
kids to juggle, I begin with only one ball.

Tell the children: Hold the ball in one
hand and toss it into your other hand.
This may be as far as you can go at this
point. That's ok; practice this movement as
often as possible. The next step is to toss the ball
up and catch it with the opposite hand. Continue with that
movement until you feel competent. The last step for this exercise is to toss
the ball high, catch it with the opposite hand, and then toss it directly across
to the opposite hand. Do this for 3 minutes.

190   Watch the Racquet

Props   A racquet and tennis ball for each pair

Experiment with directional patterns using a tennis racquet. Divide
the group into pairs or have the players choose partners.

Tell the children: This is a visual tracking game to play with a partner. Ask
your partner which way the ball will go if you hold the tennis racquet in a particular position. After she answers, toss a ball and hit the ball the same way
you held the racquet to get the answer. After doing this several times, switch
roles.

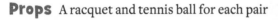

191   Soccer Stop

Props   A ball for each pair

Divide the group into pairs or have the players choose partners.

Tell the children: Stand 10 feet away from your partner and take turns rolling the ball to one another at various speeds and in different directional patterns. Trap the rolling ball with your feet, and make sure you each get to make
at least 25 traps.

192 Drop Kicks

Props A medium- to large-size ball for each pair

Divide the group into pairs or have the players choose partners.

This exercise should be done outside. Demonstrate the movement for the children first.

Tell the children: The partner holding the ball in his hands drops it to his foot and kicks it to the other player. Repeat this several times and then switch roles.

Variation To challenge the children, have them work with smaller balls or balls of different shapes.

193 Knee Bumps

Props A medium to large, soft ball for each participant

Demonstrate this movement first. This exercise is best performed outside.

Tell the children: From a standing position, hold the ball and drop it toward your knee. With proper timing, you will be able to bump the ball with your knee. Repeat this several times.

194 Tennis

Props A racquet and ball or balloon for each participant

Tell the children: The object of the game is to keep the ball or balloon from falling to the ground. Hold the racquet face up and bounce a ball on the racquet strings. Count the number of hits you can do in a row and start over if you drop the ball. Do this exercise for 3 minutes.

195 Traveling Tennis

Props A racquet and ball or balloon for each participant

Tell the children: The object of the game is to keep the ball from falling to the ground. Hold the racquet face up, bounce a ball on the racquet strings, and begin to walk. Count the number of hits you are able to make in a row and start over if you drop the ball. Do this exercise for 1 minute.

196 Tennis Dribbling

Props A racquet and ball for each participant

Tell the children: The object of the game is to repeatedly bounce the ball using the strings of the racquet. Once you get comfortable with this movement, walk around while dribbling. Count the number of dribbles you are able to do in a row and start over if you miss. Do this exercise for 1 minute.

197 Reaction Tennis

Props A wall; a racquet and ball for each participant

Tell the children: The object of this game is to hit the ball against the wall several times in a row. Count the number of hits you are able to make in a row and start over if you miss. Do this exercise for 3 minutes.

198 Moon Ball

Props A racquet and ball for each participant

Tell the children: The object of the game is to hit the ball into the air as high as you can, using the racquet strings to stay in control. Do this exercise for 5 minutes.

199 Grounder

Props A ball for each pair; 1 baseball glove per participant

Divide the group into pairs or have the players choose partners.

    Tell the children: Roll the ball at various speeds and in different directional patterns for your partner. Have her catch your grounders with a baseball glove. Do this exercise for 1 minute and then switch roles.

Circle Kicking

Props A hacky sack or foot bag for each participant

Tell the children: The object of the game is to kick the sack several times before it falls to the ground. To learn to control the sack, begin kicking it into the air with your toes and then move on to the kicking it with the instep of your foot. Do this exercise for 10 minutes.

Foot drills are an important element in mastering fundamental movements. Proper stance in starts, stops, and jumps will improve effectiveness and efficiency in most sports.

 Heel–Toe

Tell the children: Walk in a straight line, placing the heel of your right foot up against the toes of your left foot. Then step forward, placing your left heel against the toes of your right foot. Increase your speed as you feel comfortable with this movement. Do this exercise for 3 minutes.

 Side Stepping

Tell the children: From a standing position, pick up your right foot and cross it over your left foot. (The outer parts of your feet should be touching.) Then pick up your left foot, slip it out from behind the right, and move sideways. Repeat the motion to continue moving sideways. Increase your speed as you feel comfortable. Do this exercise for 1 minute.

 Shuffle

Tell the children: In a standing position, shuffle or slide your feet along the floor while moving on a forward diagonal to your right and then shuffle back to the center. Immediately shuffle on a diagonal to your left side and then come back to the center. Do this exercise for 3 minutes.

Figure-8 Shuffle

Tell the children: From a standing position, Shuffle (#203) to your right to form one half of a figure 8. Then Shuffle to your left to form the other half of a figure 8. Repeat 30 times.

Zorro Drag

Tell the children: Stand with the toes of your left foot facing straight ahead and your right foot turned out at a 45-degree angle, with its heel touching your left arch. Place your hands on your hips. Keeping your left leg straight, step forward and on a diagonal with your right foot, bending your knee to align with your ankle. Drag your right foot back to the starting position. Perform this 10 times and then switch legs.

Tire Running

Props Eight hoops or circles

This foot drill is used often in football practice.

   Tell the children: Place pairs of hoops in a line. Starting at one end of the lineup, run as fast as you can with feet stepping in the inner circle of each hoop. Do this exercise for 3 minutes.

Straddle Step

Tell the children: Stand with your feet together. Step wide with your right leg and then wide with the left leg. Immediately bring your right leg in and then bring your left leg in. This movement can be done slow or fast. Do this exercise for 3 minutes.

208 | Kangaroo Jumps

Props A small- to medium-size ball for each participant

Tell the children: Place a ball between your inner thighs. Using your inner-thigh muscles, squeeze your legs together to hold the ball in place. Squat down and jump forward, keeping the ball in place. Count the number of successful jumps you make. Do this exercise for 3 minutes.

Rhythm, Timing

In my experience with children and athletics, it is best to teach children rhythm at a young age. Rhythm doesn't just mean learning to dance. We use rhythm in basketball, tennis, gymnastics, and even in more common activities throughout our day. Rhythm may be generally defined as movement marked by the regulated succession of strong and weak elements or of opposite or different conditions. It is the recurrence or a pattern that is established in a time period. Get into the rhythm with the following exercises.

209 | Move to the Beat

Kids who love to dance and who dance well are kids who hear the beat of the music and can move different parts of their bodies with the beat. This exercise will help kids move different parts of their body separately and then bring all the parts together.

To begin, play the music.

Tell the children: Move only your head. When you feel the beat, move your shoulders. Begin with one shoulder at a time and then bring both shoulders together. Next move down to each part of the body: hands, arms, torso, and legs. Learn to move each body part separately and then bring them together. Do this exercise for 3 minutes.

210 Bounce to the Beat

Props A basketball for each participant

Tell the children: The beat is the basic unit of time in music. Beat is another word for the tempo, meter, rhythm, or groove of the music. Listen for a strong beat in your music. When you hear it, bounce a ball to the beat of the music. Do this exercise for 3 minutes.

211 Bouncing a Ball

Props A basketball for each participant

A sense of rhythm is needed in all sports. The objective of this game is to dribble a basketball with a sense of rhythm.

Tell the children: Begin by bouncing a ball to create the beat for 30 seconds. Next dribble the ball twice as fast as the beat for 30 seconds, go back to a single bounce, and then back to the "double dribble." Now add on a quick triple bounce, go back to the single, double, triple. Repeat this exercise for 3 minutes.

212 Dribble Around a Chair

Props A basketball and a chair for each participant

Tell the children: Set up a chair and dribble around it. Reverse your circle and travel backward. Repeat this exercise for 5 minutes.

213 Bouncing Basketballs

Props A basketball for each participant

Tell the children: Begin by bouncing the ball to a certain height. After you have that in control, change the rhythm by bouncing the ball higher. Keep a rhythm going at all heights. Do this exercise for 3 minutes.

214 Two-Ball Bounce

Props Two basketballs per pair

Divide the group into pairs or have the players choose partners.

    Tell the children: Partners stand about 15 feet apart. Each player has a ball, and partners bounce pass the balls to each other at the same time. Count the number of successful passes. Do this exercise for 3 minutes.

215 Nondominant Hand/ Nondominant Foot

Props A basketball and/or soccer ball for each participant

Tell the children: Dribble a basketball with only your nondominant hand, or kick a soccer ball with only your nondominant foot. Do this for 3 minutes.

216 All-Out Dribble

Props A basketball for each participant

This game is played on a basketball court. If you don't have access to a basketball court, delineate the boundaries of a court in the space you have.

    Tell the children: Starting from one end of the court, run as fast as you can to the other end of the court while dribbling the basketball. Record your time and try to beat it. Do this for 5 minutes.

217 Backward Basketball

Props A basketball for each participant

This game is played on a basketball court. If you don't have access to a basketball court, delineate the boundaries of a court in the space you have.

Tell the children: Starting from one end of the court, run backward while dribbling the basketball as fast as you can. Record your time and try to beat it. Do this for 3 minutes.

218 Basketball Balance

Props A basketball for each participant

Tell the children: Begin bouncing the basketball. Challenge yourself by standing on one leg as you dribble. Do this for 3 minutes.

219 Blindfolded Basketball

Props A basketball for each participant

Tell the children: Begin bouncing the basketball. Close your eyes and keep dribbling. Do this for 3 minutes.

220 Two-Ball Toss

Props Two balls per pair

Divide the group into pairs or have the players choose partners.

Tell the children: This exercise requires hand–eye coordination and timing. Stand about 10 feet away from your partner. Each of you holds a ball.

On "Go," toss the balls to one another at the same time. Eventually, you should try tossing the balls back and forth without having to say "Go." Do this for 3 minutes.

221 Frisbee Toss

Props A Frisbee for each pair

Throwing a Frisbee takes coordination. Divide the group into pairs or have the players choose partners.

Tell the children: In pairs, practice throwing a Frisbee. If you complete a forehand, or regular, pass, you get 1 point. Throwing a backhand pass is much more difficult. If you complete one of these, you get 2 points. The first person to reach 20 points wins.

222 Swing and a Hit

Props A skill-level-appropriate baseball and bat for each pair

Divide the group into pairs or have the players choose partners.

Tell the children: Toss a ball for your partner to hit. Practice this exercise for 15 minutes and then switch roles.

Sports Fitness

Except
as noted

What exercise is best for your child? The answer is whatever exercise they like best. For some children, the idea of playing sports is just fun; they do not realize that by playing a sport they are exercising their body.

School-age children can receive great health benefits from running shorter distances with much less risk of injury than if they run for long periods of time. If kids are doing any type of structured running, they should be fitted for appropriate running shoes.

223 Interval Runs

An interval run is a type of activity that incorporates speed and endurance in little amounts. This exercise is designed to increase or decrease intensity, not length of time. Invite your group or your whole family to go for this run. (Don't forget your dog, too.)

Tell the children: To start off, begin walking. When everyone feels ready, increase your speed from slow, to medium, to fast. Then choose someone to call out the desired level of speed. Count how many intervals you complete. Do this for 3 minutes.

224 High-Knees Running

Tell the children: Track and field athletes use this exercise as a warm-up. Run forward at a slow pace, bringing your knees waist high. Do this for 3 minutes.

225 Take a Hike

Invite your group or family for a hike in your neighborhood park. Running on a dirt path with hills is a different workout from running on concrete. Make sure everyone is prepared with sunscreen and the right clothing. If you come to a hill, take the challenge and walk or run up the hill, but when descending a hill, remember that walking is much safer than running.

Tell the children: Start out walking. Pick up the pace if the path is safe and free of roots, rocks, and other obstacles. Do this for 15 minutes.

226 Go to the Beach

Props A sandy beach or a source of at least knee-deep water; sunscreen

Take your group or family to the beach, or run in a pool. Running on sand or in water is different from running on any other surface, and it is more challenging, too. Kids will not be able to run for long periods of time on sand because their major muscles have to work harder and therefore fatigue much faster than when they run on hard surfaces.

Jumping is a skill that is used in almost every sport. It requires timing and a sense of rhythm.

227 Power Jumps

Props A mini trampoline (optional)

Tell the children: Stand with your feet hip-width apart and your arms at your sides. Bend your knees and sit back into a squat. Then pushing up using your legs to move through a standing position, jump up as high as you can. Use your arms to create momentum. As you land, bend your knees to soften the landing and lower your hips into a squat. Repeat this exercise as many times as you can.

228 Jump-Ups

Props A step or low bench for each participant

Tell the children: Stand facing a step, with your arms at your sides. Bending your left leg, place your left foot in the middle of the step. Keep your weight evenly distributed over the balls of your feet. Push off with both feet, jumping straight up as high as you can. Let your arms swing up overhead. Pause between jumps only long enough to maintain balance. Do 10 Jump-Ups with one leg and then switch legs.

229 Broad Jumps

Props Chalk or a jump rope to mark a starting line

For kids this age, I recommend this exercise be done outside. Designate the line from which the player must jump.

Tell the children: There is no running start for this game. To begin, bring your toes to the starting line. Swing your arms and, using that momentum, explode forward. Land on your feet, making sure to bend your knees. Repeat this exercise for 3 minutes.

230 180-/360-Degree Turn

This activity will help children understand how to turn while jumping, but the move can be complicated for kids this age. To make it easier, I recommend setting a visual target on each side for the children to focus on. Divide the group into pairs or have the players choose partners.

Tell the children: One player acts as the spotter while the other partner turns and faces one of the objects at his side. Jump up in the air and turn to face the other object. If you feel confident with a half turn, increase the turn until you can jump in a complete circle. To avoid getting dizzy, reverse the direction of the jump after each jump. Repeat 3 times and then switch roles with your partner.

Single-Leg Hops

Tell the children: Standing on your left leg, bend your right leg at the knee. Bring the heel of your right foot toward your bottom, and grasp and hold the ankle. Hop around the room, counting the number of successful hops. Repeat this action 25 times on each leg.

Popcorn

Tell the children: Start from a Squat position (#89), with your hands touching the floor. Explode upward, swinging your arms up overhead and landing softly in a Squat position. Repeat this exercise 25 times.

Tumbling helps children develop bi-lateral motor skills, balance, and coordination, as well as cardiovascular fitness, strength, flexibility, and agility.

Forward Rolls/ Somersaults

Divide the group into pairs or have the players choose partners.

Tell the children: Beginning in a crawl position, tuck your head into your chest and push your bottom up and over until you roll over. If necessary, assist your partner by pushing her bottom over and placing your hand on her head to keep her chin tucked under. Repeat this exercise 5 times.

234 Backward Rolls

Divide the group into pairs or have the players choose partners.

If the children are just learning to do a backward roll, demonstrate the move first and then teach the children to do it. You may want an adult—or other partner—to assist them at first so they can feel the movement.

Tell the children: Sit on the edge of a mat with your knees and chin tucked into your chest. Place your hands on either side of your head with your palms up, just above the ears. If you need help, your partner can place one hand on your head to keep it tucked and one hand on your bottom to help you lift up and over. Rock backward and forward, remaining in the tucked position. As you gain confidence, rock harder until you rock far enough back for your palms to touch the mat.

When you are comfortable, change your starting position slightly. Instead of sitting, get into the appropriate tuck while balanced on your feet. Repeat the rocking movement from the new starting point until you are ready for a break. Keep your hands in place, as protection for the head and neck. Push strongly with your hands when they touch the mat to complete the backward roll. If necessary, your partner can ease you over using your hips as a hand-hold. Practice the backward roll several times. As you gain confidence, begin the move with your hands starting on the mat, quickly bringing them up by your ears as you begin to rock backward, Do a total of 5 Backward Rolls. With practice, you will improve in both form and speed.

235 Cartwheels

When doing a cartwheel, the child moves sideways in a straight line. He keeps his back straight and places the hand of his lead side on the ground followed by the other hand. His legs pass over his body and then come down as his hands and body come up to standing. A cartwheel can be performed using one, two, or no hands. It is just a sideways motion, so it really does not matter whether the legs are straight or bent as long as the body turns over in a sideways motion.

Tell the children: Always start a cartwheel with a lunge. The stronger leg leads the lunge, and the weaker leg is in the back.

During the lunge, raise your arms straight into the air and keep your hips squared in the forward direction. Push off your front leg and place your hands shoulder-width apart or wider on the ground in front of you. As you do this, you will begin to kick your legs up and over your torso and head as the body becomes inverted. During the rotation, your legs stay straight and apart in a wide straddle. Keep your toes and feet pointed. As your first foot hits the ground, it is followed by the second foot, landing in a lunge with the weaker leg in the front and the lead leg in back. Repeat this exercise 10 times.

236 Round-Offs

Tell the children: A round-off is just like a cartwheel except that you land with your two feet together on the ground instead of one foot at a time, facing the direction from which you came. This is achieved by twisting your hands and shoulders as you place your hands on the ground. The two hands are generally placed down one after the other, kick your feet up, bring legs together and with feet together. Repeat this exercise 10 times.

237 Assisted Handstands

Prop A wall

Divide the group into pairs or have the players choose partners.

Tell the children: Ask your partner to grab your ankles in a handstand position or use a wall to help keep your balance and increase your upper-body strength. Stand about 3 feet away from the wall and lift your hands above your head. Keeping your arms straight and touching your ears, step forward, throw your hands down, and kick up.

The kick gives you more momentum. Kick one leg in front of you and take a large step forward with that leg as far as it feels comfortable to you. Keep a straight line from your fingertips to your back foot. Start to lean forward while keeping your body straight. Make sure to put a little force forward with your lunged leg and back foot.

The most common mistake is to throw your hands straight down at the ground and try to throw your legs upward. This results in a whip at the top and causes you to fall forward. Once your hands are approaching the ground, make sure to keep your arms perfectly straight. Your legs will touch the wall for support. Repeat this exercise 5 times.

238 Solo Handstands

Tell the children: Stand straight up and lift your hands above your head. Make sure your arms are straight touching your ears. Step forward and then throw your hands down. Kick up; this gives you more momentum. Kick one leg in front of you and take a large step forward with that leg as far as it feels comfortable to you. Make sure to keep your body in a straight line from your fingertips to your back foot. Start to lean forward while keeping your body straight. Make sure to put a little force forward with your lunged leg and back foot.

The most common mistake is to throw your hands straight down at the ground and try to throw your legs upward. This results in a whip at the top and causes you to fall forward. Keep straight. Once your hands are approaching the ground, make sure to keep your arms perfectly straight. Don't let your shoulders sag upward or your elbows bend. If you bend your arms, you will risk hurting yourself. If you do this right, it will help you to keep balance. When you feel most of your weight on your hands, attempt to keep the force of your weight around the base of your fingers. This allows you to push forward or backward with your hands to compensate for when you kick too hard or not hard enough. You might need to try this a few times before you find balance. Soon you will get it almost every time. Just keep all the weight on your hands. Straighten out completely. After successfully hitting the handstand, keep your head neutral and your back and legs straight. Look past your eyebrows to see your hands instead of throwing your head back, which will only result in you arching your back and hurting. Try holding your handstand for 10 seconds.

239 Hula-Hoop Twirls

Props A hula-hoop for each participant

Using a hula-hoop teaches rhythm, timing, coordination, and momentum. Begin by demonstrating the movement on your arm first. This exercise should be done outside.

Tell the children: Slide your arm inside the hula-hoop and begin to move your arm in a circle. Once you are able to keep the hoop moving on your arm for over 30 seconds, move it to your other arm.

240 Hula-Hoop Hips

Props A hula-hoop for each participant

The hula-hoop is a fun toy and a great way to exercise. This exercise should be done outside.

Tell the children: Step into the hula-hoop with both feet. Bring it up to your waist. Hold it with both hands and pull it forward so that it's resting against your back. Keep your feet planted firmly about shoulder-width apart and begin circling your hips, left, back, right, forward. With both hands, fling the hoop to the left so that its inner edge rolls in a circle around your body. This is one exercise that becomes easier with practice. Repeat this exercise 20 times.

Variation For more of a challenge, switch the direction in which the hula hoop rotates.

241 Stay Within the Lines

Props A roll of easily removable tape

Make two lines on the floor with tape. They should be 12 inches apart and 10 feet long.

Tell the children: Practice doing Forward Rolls/Somersaults (#233) within the lines. Travel through the lines 10 times.

Variation When that skill is mastered, decrease the distance between the lines an inch at a time, until the lines are only 6 inches apart.

242　Strong Upper Body

Props　Two sturdy chairs for each small group

Tell the children: Use two chairs placed shoulder-width apart to practice raising yourself up. This helps build arm strength. Have people sit in the chairs to be sure the chairs don't flip. Start with lifting yourself up about an inch. Gradually build up the height as you strengthen your muscles to prevent damaging your shoulders, elbows, or wrists. Repeat this exercise for 2 minutes.

243　Leg Splits

Tell the children: Sit on the floor with your legs straight and your toes pointed. Stretch to get your nose as close to your knees as you can. Hold this position for 30 seconds. Next, flex your feet, still holding your nose as far down as possible. After you have done this, sit in a wide straddle and attempt to place your elbows on the floor. Hold this stretch for 30 seconds and then reach your hands as far out as possible, attempting to put your nose on the floor. Again, hold this stretch for 30 seconds. Next, place either leg in front, and lunge from your knee; your rear knee is on the floor, your front foot is far in front. Hold 30 seconds and then sit back, straighten the front leg, and try to place your nose on your knees. Finally, slide as far into the split as you are able. Repeat these stretches on the other side. Hold each position for 30 seconds. NEVER bounce while stretching or push yourself when it is painful.

244　Backbends

Props　Soft pillows or a mat for each pair

Divide the group into pairs or have the players choose partners.

　Tell the children: To begin a backbend, start with your legs spread shoulder-width apart. Do this exercise slowly; don't just fall backward into a backbend. Control yourself and don't rush. If you have never tried to do this before, have a partner hold you by the waist so you can practice getting into a backbend position with support that should help you prevent your core from collapsing. Keep your arms close to your ears but not touching, and carefully place your hands on the floor. Repeat this exercise 3 times.

Note Working in pairs, one person can serve as a spotter. It is especially helpful if the partner is an adult.

Backbend Kick-Overs

Tell the children: Get into a backbend position and simply kick your strong leg up and over. Have your weaker leg just behind it. Jumping with the leg that doesn't kick over helps to put you into motion to complete this. Make sure you land with your arms up and your feet together. Repeat this exercise 3 times.

Throwing/Catching/Passing

Throwing, catching, and passing are fundamental skills that require strength and hand-eye coordination.

Side-to-Side Throw

Props A ball for each pair

Divide the group into pairs or have the players choose partners.

Tell the children: Stand side-by-side with your partner, 5 feet apart. With both hands, hold the ball out to the side away from your partner at hip height. Swing the ball across your body and throw the ball just above waist height. The other partner must catch the ball with both hands and throw the ball back to his partner using the same technique. Repeat this exercise 25 times.

247 Pass Back

Props A ball for each pair

Divide the group into pairs or have the players choose partners.

Tell the children: Sit on the floor with your knees bent and your feet flat on the floor. Lean back so that your back is at a 45-degree angle to the floor— about halfway between sitting and lying on the floor. Have your partner stand about 5 to 10 feet away. Hold the ball in front of your chest and then pass it back and forth to your partner without changing the angle of your back to the floor. Repeat this exercise 10 times and then switch positions.

248 Pass the Ball

Props A ball for each pair

Divide the group into pairs or have the players choose partners.

Tell the children: Partners lie on your backs on the floor, with the tops of your heads nearly touching. With your knees bent, place a ball between your feet and lower legs. Curl your tailbone up toward your ribcage and pass the ball over your head to your partner, using only your feet. Your partner will take the ball with her feet and both of you will return to starting position before your partner passes the ball back to you. How many passing sequences can you do? Repeat this action 20 times.

249 Backward Pass and Reach

Props A ball for each pair

Divide the group into pairs or have the players choose partners.

Tell the children: Sit with your knees bent and your feet flat on the ground. You should be back to back with your partner. Allow enough space between your bodies so that both of you can lean back and not bump heads. To begin the game, one partner holds the ball, leans back, and passes the ball overhead to the hands of his partner who is leaning back to receive it. Once your partner has the ball, she leans forward to touch it to her toes. She then leans back, brings the ball back overhead, and returns it to her partner. The partners repeat the entire sequence 25 times.

250 Jump Shots

Props A basketball for each player; a basketball hoop

This game is played on a basket-ball court. If you don't have access to a basketball court, delineate the boundar-ies of a court in the space you have.

Tell the children: Stand in various positions on the court and practice jump shots. As soon as you rebound your own ball, you must immediately shoot the basketball from that position. Do this for at least 10 minutes.

251 Scissor Jumps with Dribble

Props A variety of balls of different sizes

This is a drill that kids can do alone. It is good if they have already mastered Scissor Jumps (#124) before they start this exercise.

Tell the children: In a standing position with your feet hip-distance apart, step one foot slightly forward and start doing Scissor Jumps (#124) by quickly switching the positions of your legs. Once you feel comfortable doing that, dribble a ball while you do 50 Scissor Jumps.

Get Your Game On

any size

Except as noted

Use games as a way to get the heart pumping. Don't get caught up in technique, just be goofy and encourage movement. Before you know it, your kids will be having so much fun they won't even realize they're exercising.

 252 **Mirror Image**

pairs

Divide the group into pairs or have the players choose partners.

Tell the children: Stand facing your partner. She must copy any movement you make. Choose from running laterally, backward forward, or in a circle. Run in a squat position, with your arms up in the air, kicking your legs to the side, back, and front. Jump up high, low, forward, and backward. Walk like a duck, roll on the ground—be creative. Make at least 10 changes in movement and then switch roles.

Variation Let the children come up with ideas that you must copy.

 253 **Monkey in the Middle**

small groups

Props A soft ball for each small group

Tell the children: Get into groups of three. Two players will throw a ball back and forth while at the same time trying to keep the middle player, the "Monkey," from catching it (see the illustration on the next page). The ball may be rolled or tossed in any style (overhead, underhand, side throw, or overhand). If the player in the middle catches the ball, the player who last threw the ball and the middle player now switch positions and the game resumes. Play this game until the person playing the role of the Monkey has switched at least 10 times.

254 Graveyard Game

This game requires more than three people, so it's fun for groups or whole families. I use this game as a cool-down game, especially when you want the kids to be quiet and to calm down. Select one new player to be the graveyard keeper each time the game is played.

Tell the children: The object of the game is for the players to lie perfectly still on the floor and not to laugh as their bodies are being moved into funny positions. This game is best when played with low lighting or no lights at all. One person is the graveyard keeper, and everyone else lies on the floor. Play this game for 2 minutes.

255 Flinch

Props A soft ball and a wall

Tell the children: Designate one player to be "It." The other players line up against a wall with their arms folded. "It" stands at least 8 feet away with a soft ball. The player who is "It" will either throw the ball at one of the lined-up players or fake a throw. The players who are being thrown at have to maintain their positions with arms folded when the ball is faked, and they must catch the ball when it is actually thrown. Flinching when the ball is faked or failing to catch it when the ball is thrown earns a player a letter. The first player to spell out F-L-I-N-C-H becomes "It."

256   Marshmallow Basketball

Props   A bag of marshmallows; paper bags; tape

The more players, the more fun! This game is fun for the entire family, so be sure to include Grandma and Grandpa.

Designate at least two players to be the basketball hoop. The game can be more fun if the adults are the marshmallow hoops first. Tape the paper bags to the players' chests or chins; these are the hoops to toss the marshmallows. Everybody else gets a handful of marshmallows.

Tell the children: On "Go," start moving around the play area. Without stopping moving, the players with the marshmallows must try to toss the marshmallows into the bags of the hoop players. Once all of the marshmallows have been tossed, count the amount of marshmallows that each hoop collected.

257   Tug of War

Props   A long rope; a handkerchief or bandana

This is a great game anytime.

Tell the children: Mark a line on the ground. Next, get an appropriate-size rope and tie a handkerchief in the center of the rope so you can see which team is pulling the most. Divide your group into teams and arrange participants evenly on either side of the rope. The object of the game is to pull the other team across the line in the middle.

Variation   If you want to have some fun with this game, try playing the game over a small mud hole, baby swimming pool, or wet sand. This game can be played by as few as two people, too.

258   Flying Saucers

Props   A Frisbee for each player

Divide kids into two teams. Give each player a Frisbee. Designate the amount of time for which the game will be played: I recommend approximately 30 minutes of game time.

Tell the children: The object of this game is to catch as many Frisbees as you can. The teams must stand about 20 feet apart. On "Go," players will begin throwing the discs to the other team. When play ends, the player who has caught the most discs wins.

259 Teamwork

Props A Frisbee for each group

Tell the children: Line up in groups of six or so and have a Frisbee placed 10 feet in front each of the lines, with the players facing it. The players need to be well placed, at least an arm-length apart.

On "Go!" the left-most player runs out, picks up the disc, and throws it to the first (right-most) player. The right-most player throws it back to the receiver and then sits down. The receiver then moves on to the second player from the right and so forth until the original thrower has finished throwing the Frisbee to each member on his team. If a player has to retrieve a disc, he must return to his place before throwing the return pass. The team that is first to get all of its players to finish and sit down wins.

260 Frisbee Golf

Props Frisbees or flying discs; a goal marker

This game is a fun way to teach children of this age group the game of golf. You don't have to be a member of a golf course to play this game. You can play it in your own backyard. Just put a flat disc or any other type of flat marker on the ground to represent the holes. If you don't have enough space to play 18 holes, you can either place as many goals as you can fit in your yard, or move the goal each round after each player has finished the round. You can play as teams or play individually.

Tell the children: Frisbee golf is played like regular golf, but instead of using golf balls and clubs you throw a Frisbee. To begin the game the first player must throw the Frisbee toward the goal. Each player then takes a turn. Wherever the Frisbee lands is where you play your next shot. After everyone has had their first throw, the player with the Frisbee furthest away takes the next throw and so forth. Each time a player throws a Frisbee, whether or not it hits the goal they get one point, and they must continue throwing their Frisbee until they hit the goal. The object of this game is to have the lowest score for 18 "holes" of Frisbee Golf.

261 Frisbee Soccer

Props A Frisbee; 2 goals

This game can be played on a soccer field.

Divide the players in to two teams. Designate the amount of time for which the game will be played.

Tell the children: This game is played much like the game of soccer. In this game, however, you are not allowed to run with the disc, but the disc is allowed to touch and roll along the ground. Once the Frisbee is on the ground, either team may pick it up. If two players pick up the Frisbee simultaneously, then the offensive team retains possession. The points are awarded when one team throws the Frisbee into the opponents' goal (net). Play this game for 30 minutes.

262 Frisbee Baseball

Props A Frisbee; 3 bases

Divide the players into two teams.

Tell the children: The game is set up and played just like baseball. The only difference is that you throw and catch a Frisbee instead of a baseball. As a "batter," you must throw the Frisbee from home plate; you must re-throw if it is a foul or doesn't travel at least 10 feet. Three fouls, and you are out. You are also out if your throw is caught. As a "runner," you are out if the Frisbee beats you to the base you are running toward. The batting team gets a run each time a runner reaches home plate. As in baseball, teams switch roles when the team at bat has 3 outs.

Note It is recommended that this game be played for 15 minutes so each child has a chance to play every position.

263 Frisbee Volleyball

Props A Frisbee; a marker; a volleyball net

The set up and the rules of the game are just like volleyball.

Divide the players in two teams. Decide which team will serve first. The other team becomes the receiving team. Use a marker to designate the back of the court; this is where the players serve from.

Tell the children: The server throws the Frisbee, and the opponents must catch the Frisbee and throw it back over the net. If the receiving team drops the Frisbee or takes more than 3 passes to get it over the net, the serving team scores a point. That team continues serving until a serve goes out of bounds or that team's players fail to get the Frisbee back over the net. Then the other team becomes the serving team. The game is played to 15 points.

264 Frisbee Basketball

Props A Frisbee; 2 goals

Divide the players into two teams. Designate the goals for each team. (The goals should not be basketball hoops as the Frisbee will get stuck in them.) Good goals for this game are best established on the ground, such as in the form of an end zone, like a soccer net or between 2 cones.

Tell the children: Each team has four players, and a total of eight players are on the field at one time. Divide the field into four sections. One member from each team will be at the offensive end zone and at the defensive end zone, and the other two positions divide the rest of the field. These players will stay within their designated area for the entire game or until a point is scored, and then they can be reassigned to a different position. The Frisbee must be thrown from player to player to make a goal. Only the defensive player in that section can defend or try to catch the Frisbee against the offensive player. After a player throws the Frisbee in to the goal, the game starts again, attacking the opposite goal. Play this game for 30 minutes.

265 Touch Football Frisbee

Props A Frisbee; end zone markers

Divide the players into two teams.

The playing field should be rectangular, with an end zone at each end. Anything outside the playing area is out of bounds. Choose a method of deciding a winner by limiting either playing time or points scored. For example, the winning team could be the one with the highest score at the end of an hour or the first team to score 5 points. Play with two teams with equal numbers of players; seven on each side is best. Flip a coin to decide which team will begin playing offense.

Tell the children: Play begins with the defensive team in their end zone and the offensive team lined up on their end zone line. The defensive team throws the Frisbee to the other team to begin the game. If a throw goes out of bounds, then the receiving team has a choice of putting the Frisbee in play from the sideline where it went out of bounds or at the center of the field nearest to where it went out of bounds. Once a player catches or picks up the disc, she must come to a stop and have one foot planted as a pivot until she throws the Frisbee to another player. Hand-offs are not permitted.

The Frisbee goes back to the defense when the offense doesn't complete a pass, the pass is dropped by the offense, the pass is knocked down by the defense, or the defense catches a pass. In these cases, the defense now becomes the offense team. The offense team takes possession of the Frisbee at the point where the Frisbee lies or where the player came to a stop after catching it. Play is continuous until a score is made. Goals are scored by a team successfully completing a pass to a player located in the defensive end zone. After a score, the teams switch their direction of attack.

266 Knock 'Em Down

Props A Frisbee and 1 bottle for each player

Divide the players into two teams. Line up the teams, facing each other, with each player having a bottle in front of them.

Tell the children: The object of this game is to knock over the other team's bottles. You must throw the Frisbee from behind your bottle, and you may throw only when your bottle is upright. Each player starts with

three *"lives."* When your bottle is knocked over, you
lose a life. When you have no lives left, you are out of
the game and must sit down.

During play, you (or any other player) may retrieve a Frisbee from the "no-man's land," which
is the area between the teams, but you cannot go
behind enemy lines. No goal-tending is allowed,
and a receiver cannot touch a moving Frisbee until
it passes the line of bottles.

267 Wimpy Throw

Prop A Frisbee

Divide the kids into 2 teams, standing about 8 feet apart.

Tell the children: One team throws a really soft throw to the receiving
team, and players must try to catch it with one hand. The Frisbee must be
thrown so that it reaches the other team in the area between the head and
knees or it does not count and must be thrown again.

You or any receiving team member may touch the Frisbee before it is
caught, but no two hands or players may touch it at the same time. Also, you
may not "trap" the Frisbee, which happens when the disc is trapped between
your hand and another part of your body. You keep the Frisbee alive by hitting it with any body part as long as it is not a trap, and the receiving team may
move anywhere they like to make a play on the disc. After the disc hits the
ground or is caught, the receiving team then serves the Frisbee. Score a point
for a successful catch. The first team to get 11 points wins.

268 Five Hundred

Prop A Frisbee

Divide the players into two teams. Teams stand approximately 25
feet apart.

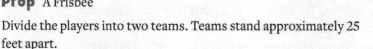

Tell the children: One team throws a high Frisbee to the other group. If someone catches it, the player who catches the Frisbee scores 100 points. Now that group throws a high throw back, and the other team gets a chance to score points. The winner is the first person on a team to score 500 points.

269 Consistency Drill

Props A Frisbee; markers for boundaries

Divide the players into 2 teams. Each team works independently but moves around the same area as their opponents. Designate the amount of time for which the game will be played.

Form a square with the four markers. Alternate the players, team 1, team 2, and have them stand inside the markers.

Allow approximately 15 minutes to play this game.

Tell the children: The object of this game is to retain possession of the Frisbee for as long as possible by throwing it to your teammates. Your opponents may not block any shots. Each time a throw-and-catch combination is successful, that team receives one point. If a team player does not catch the Frisbee or the Frisbee goes out of bounds, then the other team takes possession of the Frisbee. When the time is up, the team with the highest score wins.

270 Accuracy Frisbee

Props A Frisbee; 2 goals

Divide the players in to 2 teams. Establish 2 scoring goals, separated by about 25 feet.

Tell the children: The object of this game is to try to score a point by throwing the Frisbee into the opponent's goal. The game ends when a team reaches 10 points or after 15 minutes passes.

Cleaning House

Props Two Frisbees; 2 goals

Divide the players into two teams. Establish two scoring goals, these are called "boxes." The playing area, or "court," can be outdoors or indoors and should be large enough for players to move around in order to catch the Frisbee. If you have a large number of children playing, the space should be large enough so the kids don't bump into each other.

Tell the children: A pair of players stand in each "box"; each has one Frisbee. Each team serves simultaneously and aims to land the Frisbee in the other team's "court." If the Frisbee lands outside the court or rolls out, the receiving team gets a point. If the Frisbee lands inside the court and stays in, then the throwing team gets a point. If the receiving team catches the Frisbee, they can throw it back. If the receiving team drops the Frisbee, the throwing team gets a point. If a team is touching both Frisbees at once, that is a "double," and the other team scores 2 points. After a point is scored, the Frisbees are returned to each team and other players serve. Change ends every 5 points. The winning team is the first to reach 11 points.

 Chinese Jump Rope

Props A Chinese jump rope for each small group

You will need a Chinese jump rope to play this game. You can buy them at toy stores or sporting good stores. You will need at least three kids for this game.

Tell the children: Begin with the rope around the ankles of two children.

If you are the person playing the game, jump inside the rope with both feet. Next, jump out of the rope with both legs straddling each outside rope. Next, jump up and straddle the right side of the rope and then jump up and straddle the left side of the rope. Next, jump up and land with both feet on the ropes. Finally, jump off the ropes and crisscross your legs. This will crisscross the rope so that your legs are inside of an "X." Then jump out and straddle the rope.

If you miss the rope or jump in the wrong sequence, you are out. Or if you are trying to land on it and miss, you are out. With each sequence you say, "in, out, side, side, on, crisscross."

273   Cat and Mouse

Prop A large bed sheet

Tell the children: Two players are chosen; one is the cat, and the other is the mouse. The other players sit on the ground holding on to the sheet. The mouse goes under the sheet and crawls around on hands and knees, while the other players hold the sheet and shake it up and down. The cat is also on her hands and knees and tries to locate the mouse. If she touches the mouse, she becomes the mouse and a new cat is chosen. Play this game for 30 minutes or until each player has a chance to be the cat or the mouse.

274   Treasure Map Active Games

Props Colored paper; small objects such as plastic toys

Divide the group into pairs or have the players choose partners.

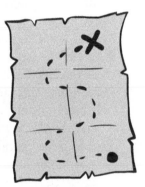

Kids love activities that engage the brain and their muscles. This game has both clues for their brains and physical activity as the teams move from one clue to the next.

Divide the players into teams, with each team taking a different color. The clues will be printed on colored paper, representing each team's colors. The team cannot split up; players must remain with their team at all times.

To design the game, you will need a list of exercises mixed with a riddle and a collection of small objects. You can use any exercise within this book, each team should have a different type of exercise to reach each clue location.

Tell the children: Teams use clues to go from location to location. A new clue for each team will be at each location. Teams may pick up only their clue at each location. Players must not hide, touch, or disturb any of the clues intended for other teams. When the team finds their clue, they must collect it and any objects waiting there for them, read the clue's instructions on how to move to the next clue, and move on. When time is up or when a team has finished collecting each one of their clues, they must go to the designated finishing location and turn in the objects to solve the mystery or riddle.

Here is an example: "The Stolen Crown Jewels"

Help the detective collect the clues to locate the stolen jewels. Collect several colored plastic pieces that resemble jewels. Hide a jewel per team at each location. Select the locations in which you will place the jewels and the clues and create riddles and the type of exercise the team must perform to get to their clue.

Clue #1.   Hippity Hop to a dog's favorite spot.
Clue #2.   Jumping Jack flash to a place that goes splash.
Clue #3.   Tootsie Roll, rolls down a hill.

275 Scavenger Hunt

Props Nature treasures like a twig with a V shape, a red leaf, a worm, a wild-flower, a rock as big as your fist, a four-leaf clover, something someone left behind, a piece of paper, etc.; lists of clues for each group

This is a team game. In advance, write a list of all the items to be found and create clues to help players find the objects. This game is a fun game to be played in a park or on the beach, or in the woods or even on a hiking trip. Depending on the number of players involved, the more objects you have, the better the game. This is a timed game, so on your command, send out the groups and let the fun begin. Allow approximately 30 minutes for this game— you can make this game longer or shorter depending on the number of clues and objects you hide.

Tell the children: I will give each team a list of clues. These clues can be riddles about the location where the objects are hidden. When I say "Go!" read the instructions and go in search of the objects. The group that has discovered the most "treasures" when time is up wins.

Note If you have a crowd with younger and older kids, create two different sets of objects and clues.

276 Opposite Attraction

One player is selected to be the caller. The rest of the players line up one behind another. Allow approximately 15 minutes for this game.

Tell the children: The caller will toss the ball and yell either "Catch" or "Kick." The first person in line will do the opposite of what the caller says. If the caller yells "Catch," the player must kick the ball. If the caller yells "Kick," the player must catch the ball. If the player misses the ball or does the wrong action, then she must move to the back of the line, and play continues. If the player does the right thing, she becomes the caller.

 Bocce Ball

Props A bocce ball set

The great thing about open bocce is that it can be played almost anywhere you can find open space. This includes grassy surfaces such as a front lawn or backyard, dirt surfaces, sandy surfaces such as the beach, and even paved surfaces like parking lots. The places that you can play bocce are limited only by your imagination. Bocce is played with eight large balls and one smaller ball (called the pallino). The game can be played with two, four, or eight players. Divide the bocce balls evenly between the number of players. You will notice that your bocce ball set has balls with several different colors or designs. Ideally, each bocce player will use balls from the set that are unique in design or color from all the other balls in play. This is helpful in distinguishing one player's bocce balls from those of another player.

Tell the children: The purpose of the game is to get your bocce balls as close as possible to the pallino, the smaller ball. Choose a player to throw the pallino. After the pallino is thrown, the same player will throw his first bocce ball. After the first player has thrown his first bocce ball, he is considered "inside," because his ball is closer to the pallino than any of the competitors' balls. All other players are considered "outside." Whenever a player is considered "inside," he will forfeit his turn throwing bocce balls. All "outside" players will take turns throwing their bocce balls until one of theirs gets closer to the pallino than the "inside" player.

After all players have thrown their bocce balls, the player who is "inside" will be awarded points. One point will be awarded to this player for every ball that is closer to the pallino than his closest competitor's ball. After the points are awarded, that game is done. Start a new game by electing a new person to throw the pallino and to throw the first bocce ball. A game is won when a player reaches 13 points. Play as many frames as necessary until a player reaches this point level.

Variation Playing bocce on a surface with hills or slopes adds a new element of strategy to the game.

Tag Games

Kids at this age love playing games with their friends and families. Tag is a great way to blend exercise and fun.

278 Freeze Tag

whole group

This is a chasing game in which one person is "It." The player who is "It" chases the other players, tagging and "freezing" them. Put a time limit on each game and give every player the opportunity to be "It."

Tell the children: The object of the game is for the player who is "It" to tag as many players as she can within a time period. If a player is tagged, he must freeze in the exact position he was in when tagged. If an untagged player touches a frozen player, he is thawed and can run freely again.

Variation Have the children suggest a theme for this game. For example, each player pretends to be an animal or a cartoon character and stays in character during play.

279 British Bulldog

whole group

Tell the children: Designate three players to be the British bulldogs and create an area for the "dog pen." The other players stand at either end of the field; the three "bulldogs" stand in the middle. When the bulldogs begin barking, the other players must run to the opposite side of the field without being touched. Any players who are touched are put in the dog pen and must wait for a new game.

Flashlight Tag

Prop A flashlight

Played at night, this game mixes the popular games of hide-and-seek and tag.

Tell the children: The person who is "It" waits at the "jail" counting to a high number while everyone else hides. With a flashlight, "It" searches for the others, who may be switching hiding spots. The flashlight must remain on at all times and may not be covered. When "It" spots someone, he must use the flashlight to get a close enough look at the person to identify the player and call out her name. Each time a player is correctly identified that person goes to "jail" to wait until everyone has been caught. The first person caught then becomes "It."

Variations

- If a person is caught, he is given the flashlight and immediately become "It."

- More than one person (or a team) is "It." With this configuration, people who are not "It" can tag other players free from jail. One person who is "It" may stay near the jail to guard it.

Note Players will find ways to improve their play. One such strategy is to watch where "It" has already searched and then move to that hiding spot. Players may also want to follow quietly behind "It."

Attack or Retreat

Props A quarter to toss; 2 designated safety zones

Divide the kids into two equal teams. Each team will need a captain. Teams line up about 5 feet apart, facing each other. Designate a safety zone approximately 25 feet behind each of the teams.

Tell the children: Team leaders, called captains, stand with their teams. The captains will alternate tossing the coin. If the coin lands heads up, the captain who tossed the coin will yell "Attack!" If the coin is tails, the captain will yell "Retreat!" When one team attacks, players will chase the other team's players, trying to tag as many as possible. Players on the retreating team quickly turn and run to their safety zone. Tagged players sit on the side of the playing field until all players of one team are captured. The team with players left wins.

282 Imitation Tag

This game is great fun, especially if an adult starts off the game as the chaser.

Tell the children: One person will be the "chaser." The chaser chooses a movement to be imitated by all the other players, such as walking in slow motion, running backward, skipping, hopping, leaping like a frog, crawling like a crab, or anything else he can imagine. The chaser runs after the other players in the chosen style, trying to tag them. Anyone who is tagged also becomes a chaser, and the game continues until all players are tagged.

283 Snake in the Gutter

Depending on the number of players, designate at least three kids as the snakes. Have the snakes form the gutter by standing in a line with wide spaces between them, facing the rest of the kids, who should be at a distance.

Tell the children: A leader or player yells, "Snake in the gutter!" You have to try to run through the gutter without being tagged by a snake. If you get tagged, you are now a snake and must stay in the gutter, too. Anyone who makes it through can make another run through the gutter. The game continues until everyone has been caught.

284 Ball Tag

Prop A vinyl ball

Tell the children: One person is "It," and the other players run to avoid being hit by the ball he throws. "It" stands in the center of the field; the players are along one side. On "Go," all players must run to the other side, trying to avoid being hit by the ball. "It" must throw the ball at the players below the waist to tag them. If a person is hit, then she becomes "It."

285 Follow-the-Leader Tag

This game is a fun game for adults to play along with the kids. It requires partnerships.

Divide the group of kids into pairs (or have the players choose partners), and one of the pair will be the leader. Designate one person to be "It."

Tell the children: One person is "It." Everyone else is in pairs; one of the pair will be the "leader," and one will be the "follower." The follower will get as close as possible to the leader without touching the leader. The person who is "It" will yell out a motion to follow such as skipping, running, walking backward, or jumping, and the follower must copy the leader as they chase "It." When a pair tags "It," the leader of that pair becomes "It." All other leaders and followers switch roles, and play starts again.

286 I Can't See

pairs

Props A blindfold and foam balls for each pair

Divide the group into pairs or have the players choose partners. One partner in the pair will wear a blindfold and carry a set number of balls, and the other partner will guide her.

Tell the children: The object of the game is to have the blindfolded partner throw foam balls at other blindfolded players while at the same time avoiding getting hit by other pairs' balls. The partner without the blindfold can give the blindfolded partner

instructions, but she can only use her voice. When a blindfolded player is hit twice, the pair is "out" and must head to the sidelines to watch the rest of the game. Kids can help the blindfolded partner defend himself by telling him when to duck or when to move in a particular direction. Do this for 3 minutes and then switch roles.

Elbow Tag

Designate one chaser and one runner, and divide the group into pairs or have the players choose partners.

Tell the children: Link elbows with your partner and stand in a very large circle, leaving at least 10 feet between all of the pairs. The chaser will run after the runner; however, if the runner wants to escape and take a rest from running, she simply runs toward one of the standing couples and links elbows with one of the pair to make a threesome. In this game, two is company but three is a crowd: When the runner latches on, the one member of the pair whose arm she did not take must break away and become the runner, until he dashes to yet another pair for safety.

Variation To add an additional element of fun, the adult or leader can call "Switch!" at which point the runner and the chaser switch roles.

Tag! You're Out

Props A ball; 2 bases (trees, bags, cones, a pillow)

This game can be played with one or multiple runners. Set up two bases about 20 feet apart. Two kids are chosen to be "It," one for each base, and the other kids divide and go to the bases. The kids who are "It" try to tag the other players with the ball as they run to the bases. Allow approximately 15 minutes to play this game.

Tell the children: The object of the game is to run to the bases without being tagged by the ball. The game begins with the two kids who are "It" tossing the ball to each other. The base runners try to run from one base to the other without being tagged by the ball. The ball must be in a player's hand to tag a runner. If you are tagged, you become "It," and the game continues.

Races and Relay Races

Relay games are particularly fun for kids and help them learn about team-work. Competition can bring out the best effort in people.

 ## Animal Relay

Divide the players into two teams. The teams form two lines with equal numbers of people in each. Adults will assign players a type of animal to imitate.

Tell the children: The first players on each team are the same animal; the second players are the same animal, too, but different from the first players, and so on. On "Go," the first player acts like her animal, running, hopping, crawling, slithering, galloping...to the goal line and back. She then tags the next player. The next player then acts like his animal and so on until one team is finished and sitting down. The first team with everyone sitting down wins this race.

 ## Beanbag Race

Props One beanbag for each participant

Designate a starting line, a finish line, and a leader to call out directions. Players race to the finish line, following the directions they hear and carrying their beanbags. This game doesn't need to have a winner; it's just fun!

Tell the children: Place your beanbag either on your head or between your legs. The object of the game is to reach the finish line with your beanbag in place. On "Go," the leader will tell you to walk, run, hop, gallop, skip, crawl, walk backward, or anything else that she can imagine. Move toward the finish line, performing that movement and carrying your beanbag.

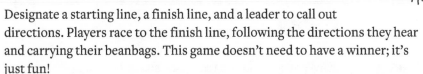

291 Potato-Sack Race

whole group

Props One sack for each participant

Designate a starting line, a finishing line, and a leader to call out directions.

Tell the children: One person will say, "Go." You must step into your sack and, while holding on to it, hop as fast as you can to the finish line.

292 Wheelbarrow Race

pairs

Tell the children: Each team consists of one player in the Wheelbarrow position (#67) and another player acting as the pusher who picks up the ankles of the wheelbarrow and supports his body. On "Go," your wheelbarrow partner moves forward on his hands while you hold tightly onto his ankles. Race to the finish line.

293 Egg-and-Spoon Relay

whole group

Props An egg (hard boiled) for each team; one spoon for each participant

Divide the players into two teams. Give every player a spoon and each team a hard-boiled egg. Each teammate runs one leg of the race.

Tell the children: Each child takes a turn carrying her team's egg on the spoon from the starting line to a turnaround point and back again. Once a player is finished, she passes the egg to the next teammate in line. If you drop the egg, you must stop and retrieve it. The team that finishes the race first wins the game.

294 Hula-Hoop Race

Props A hula-hoop for each team

Divide group into two teams. Each team join hands to form a circle.

Tell the children: Loop a hula-hoop over your arm. Without letting go of the other player's hands, step into and through the hoop so it rests on your other arm. Next slide the hoop onto the next player's arm, and she must repeat the maneuver. Whichever team can pass the hoop all the way around the circle first, without letting go of each others' hands, is the winner.

Variation If you have a large group of players you can turn this game in to a competition by forming two straight lines with the same amount of players. The game is played the same as mentioned above, but the team that finishes first wins that round. Mix up the players and allow 15 minutes for this game.

A family that plays together, stays together. It is so important to plan ahead to have quality family time. Years from now you won't remember much about the day-to-day events of work, school, and activities, but your family will remember the "traditions" that kept you close. And they will probably plan those kinds of fun family nights for their families in the future.

295 Crack the Whip

Though often played on ice while wearing skates in the winter, this game is much safer when played on grass.

Tell the children: Hold hands with the other players and form a line. Once everyone has linked hands, begin running. If you are the person at one end of the line—the tail of the "whip"—you will find that you change directions quickly and with a lot more force than players closer to the front. The longer the tail, the harder it is to hold on. If you or any of the players at the end fall off the tail, try to get back on, perhaps in a position closer to the front.

296 Spud

Prop A ball

This outdoor game is a lot of fun. Every player gets a number and crowds around the person who is "It" for that round.

Tell the children: If you are "It," you toss the ball into the air, and the other players run away. As the ball reaches the top of its toss, call out another player's number and then you run away too. The player whose number was called runs back to catch the ball (or chase after it if it is bouncing around). When that person has the ball, he yells, "Spud!" Everyone else freezes. The person with the ball throws it at one of the players. If he hits someone, the new player gets a letter (first *S*, then *P*, then *U*, then *D*) and is now "It." If he misses his target, he is "It" for the next round.

297 Shadow Tag

This is a great game for adults to play with children because an adult's shadow may be bigger and easier to tag. It must be played on a sunny day.

Tell the children: In this version of tag, you tag each other's shadows with your feet instead of tagging each other's bodies.

298 Ball in the Air

Props A ball for each pair

If the children like volleyball, they will love this game. Divide the group into pairs or have the players choose partners.

Tell the children: The game begins when you or your partner hits the ball into the air with your hands. You can use other body parts to hit the ball, but you can hit it only twice in a row before passing it to your partner. Try to keep the ball aloft as long as possible. The team who can get the most hits before the ball falls is the winner.

Double Jump

Prop An extra-long jump rope

You need four players for this game.

Tell the children: Have two people hold the ends of the jump rope. Two other players will stand with their right feet parallel to the jump rope, which is on the ground. To begin, swing the jump rope just side to side. The players who are jumping will jump with both feet each time the rope passes their feet. Once they have mastered the low swing, it is time to circle the rope over their heads to begin the jump. Each time the rope circles, the players will jump with both feet over the rope. This game does take time to learn, so allow 10 minutes for each pair of jumpers.

 Target Practice

Props Plastic bottles; a Frisbee

Set up a series of plastic bottles. Based on the throwing abilities of the players, designate a line and have participants stand behind it.

Tell the children: Stand with other players behind the designated line. Take turns tossing the Frisbee toward the bottles. The person who knocks over the most bottles wins.

 Socball

Props A football; 2 cones for goals

Set up two goals—one at each end of your field—and divide the group into two teams. Teams move the ball down the field to score. In this crazy game, players kick or throw the football as if in a soccer game. They work their way down the field with the ball toward the goal, which, in another twist, has no goalie.

Tell the children: Move the ball down the field to score by throwing the ball or kicking the ball from one teammate to another toward the goal. When a team successfully gets the ball into their opponents' goal they receive one point.

302 Back-to-Back Race

Divide the group into pairs. Designate a starting line and a finishing line.

Tell the children: With your partner, race from the starting line to the finish line, remaining back to back, with your arms linked, for the entire run.

Start in a back-to-back squat position. Stand up together and begin walking or running toward the finishing line, with one partner moving forward and the other partner moving backward. If you fall, you get into the back-to-back squat again, stand up, and continue.

303 Dead Ball

Props Lots of balls of various sizes and shapes; a timer

One person is the caller, and everyone else plays the game. The caller sets the timer for 3 minutes (the maximum length of the game) and starts it while calling "Live ball" (see below).

Tell the children: The object of the game is to work as a group to keep all balls moving. On the words "Live ball!" all players must throw all the balls into the air. As the balls land, players must throw, bounce, or kick the balls to keep them moving. If the caller sees a ball that is not moving, the caller will yell "Dead ball" and count down from 5. Players must find the nonmoving ball and get it moving once again. If the caller counts down to 1, the game is over, and the timer is stopped.

Circuit Station/Interval Training

Interval training is a type of physical activity that involves alternating high-intensity workouts with periods of low activity or rest. For children of this age group, it is important to have many stations and to be sure that the children are performing each movement properly.

Circuit training is a good activity because it allows you to create your own stations and incorporate any and all components of fitness: aerobics, strength training, flexibility, balance, and endurance. Write your stations on cards. Place the cards in a large circle either inside or outside. You can use them in your house or classroom or take them to the park, where you can incorporate the equipment you may find at the park into your workout.

Circuit Training (Indoors)
1. Running in Place (#119)
2. Biceps Curls (#61)
3. Running in Place (#119)
4. Wall Push-Ups (#59)
5. Running in Place (#119)
6. Scissor Jumps (#124)
7. Running in Place (#119)
8. Heel to Bottom (#104)
9. Running in Place (#119)
10. Donkey Kicks (#128)

Aerobic Training Station (Indoor/Outdoor)
1. Lunges alternating right and left leg (#92)
2. Roll Like a Ball (#55)
3. Jumping Jacks (#126)
4. Biceps Curls (#61)
5. Skipping (#127)
6. Crab Walk (#102)
7. Running in Place (#119)
8. Forward Rolls/Somersaults (#233)
9. High Kicks (#129)
10. Donkey Kicks (#128)

Aerobic Training Station (Swimming Pool)

1. Running in Place (#119)
2. Arm Circles (#4), underwater
3. swim to one side and back
4. jump up high
5. stand on one leg for balance
6. High Kicks (#129)
7. run backward in the pool
8. Triceps Push-Aways (#74)
9. hang onto side of pool and kick your feet
10. run in a circle

Aerobic Training Station (Indoor)

1. Running in Place (#119)
2. Jumping Jacks (#126)
3. Trunk Twists (#47)
4. wide-leg Running in Place (#119)
5. Squats (#89)
6. V Sits (#32)
7. High Kicks (#129)
8. Throwing a Ghost Ball (#70)
9. Stairway Push-Ups (#69)
10. Sit-Ups (#52)

Aerobic Training Station (Arms Only)

1. Goal Post (#38)
2. Throwing a Ghost Ball (#70)
3. Triceps Push-Aways (#74)
4. Pointer (#34)
5. Stairway Push-Ups (#69)
6. Overhead Presses (#72)
7. Beginner Push-Ups (#58)
8. Arm Circles (#4)
9. Crab Kicks (#103)
10. Biceps Curls (#61)

Aerobic Training Station (One Minute per Station)

1. Running in Place (#119)
2. run forward and backward 10 steps; keep repeating
3. Punching Arms (#71)
4. run to a cone and jump 10 times; repeat
5. while child is running, toss a ball for her to catch; repeat

6. Roll Like a Ball (#55)
7. Crab Walk (#102)
8. Basketball Hook (#75)
9. High Kicks (#129)
10. Windmill (#36)

Aerobic Training Station (20 Reps Each Station)
1. Jumping Jacks (#126)
2. Sit Kicks (#95)
3. Lunge (#92)
4. Tuck Jumps (#136)
5. High Kicks (#129)
6. Bottom Walking (#101)
7. Stairway Push-Ups (#69)
8. Hula Hips (#42)
9. Running in Place (#119)
10. Speed Skate (#137)

Aerobic Training Station (Baseball)
1. Throwing a Ghost Ball (#70)
2. Running in Place (#119)
3. Skipping (#127)
4. Overhead Stretch (#40)
5. Tuck Jumps (#136)
6. hit a ball off a T-ball stand
7. run to one goal and back
8. throw a ball in the air and catch it
9. Frog Jump (#130)
10. High Kicks (#129)

Aerobic Training Station (Just Legs)
1. Heel to Bottom (#104)
2. High Kicks (#129)
3. Elbow–Knee (#135)
4. Scissor Jumps (#124)
5. Running in Place (#119)
6. Biceps Curls (#61)
7. Lunge (#92)
8. Frog Jump (#130)
9. Knee Taps (#131)
10. Donkey Kicks (#128)

Aerobic Training Station (Olympic Events)
1. long jumps
2. Scissor Jumps (#124)
3. bounce a ball around a chair
4. Imaginary Bicycle (#99)
5. throw balls into a laundry basket
6. throw a Frisbee
7. hop on one leg, switch
8. kick a ball for distance
9. jump over obstacles
10. Hula Hips (#42)

Obstacle Courses

Have the children help design an obstacle course. Think of each activity or obstacle in terms of gross motor skills such as running, jumping, hopping, and throwing. Plan about five to seven activities within your obstacle course. Don't make the obstacle too difficult to understand; it should be simple and fun with a little instruction to be navigated quickly. If the children are interested in a particular sport or want to try out a new sport, build an obstacle course around the skills needed for that particular sport.

Outdoor Baseball Obstacle Course
1. Run to a designated area and back 4 times.
2. Throw a ball at a target 10 times.
3. Hit 10 balls with a baseball bat.
4. Stand and squat, 10 times.
5. Toss a ball in the air and catch it, 10 times.
   Repeat the entire sequence 3 times.

Outdoor Basketball Obstacle Course
1. Run to one goal, tag it, and immediately run back to starting position.
2. Jump up and down 10 times.
3. Toss a ball into a basket 10 times (vary the heights of baskets).
4. Dribble a ball around cans.
5. Bounce a ball off of a wall, catch it, and bounce it again, 10 times.
   Repeat the entire sequence 3 times.

Outdoor Soccer Obstacle Course
1. Kick a ball as far as you can 10 times.
2. Run from one goal to another 4 times.
3. Dribble a ball, using feet, around cans.
4. Kick a ball into a goal 10 times.
5. Run 10 steps in one direction, change direction, and run 10 more steps.
   Repeat the entire sequence 3 times.

Outdoor Gymnastics Obstacle Course
1. Forward Rolls/Somersaults (#233) 5 times.
2. Perform a headstand (assistance may be required).
3. Walk across a balance beam (a long piece of wood on the ground).
4. High Kicks (#129) 20 times.

5. Donkey Kicks (#128) 10 times.
   Repeat the entire sequence 3 times.

Indoor Dance Obstacle Course
1. Leap10 times.
2. Do Heel to Bottom (#104) 10 times.
3. Swing arms in a circle overhead 10 times.
4. Move laterally, step to the side, step together. Move 10 times in one direction and then repeat moving in the other direction.
5. Do Hula-Hoop Hips (#240) 10 times.
   Repeat the entire sequence 3 times.

Multi-Sport Obstacle Course
1. Ride a bike to a goal and back.
2. Shoot balls into a basket 25 times.
3. Jump Rope, Both Feet Low (#120) for a count of 50 jumps.
4. Run to a goal.
5. Swim for 10 minutes.
   Repeat the entire sequence 3 times.

Obstacle Course to Improve Hand–Eye Coordination
1. Pass a ball from one person to another at various heights for 30 seconds.
2. Bounce a ball for one minute.
3. Dribble a tennis ball with a tennis racquet for 1 minute.
4. Throw a ball into the air and catch it 10 times.
5. Throw a soft ball against a wall and catch it 10 times.
   Repeat the entire sequence 3 times.

Obstacle Course for the Pool
1. Swim to one side of the pool and back.
2. Jump up and down 10 times.
3. Run backward across the pool.
4. Alternate high leg kicks from one end of the pool to the other.
5. Using a kickboard flutter, kick to one end of the pool.
   Repeat the entire sequence 3 times.

An Example of an Indoor Obstacle Course
1. Drape a blanket over two chairs for crawling under.
2. Dribble a ball around soup cans.
3. Place tape on the floor for a long jump.
4. Go up and down a set a stairs.
5. Toss balls into a laundry basket.

6. Run to a wall and back.
7. Jump up high and leave a sticky note on the wall for measurement.
   Repeat the entire sequence 3 times.

An Example of an Outdoor Obstacle Course

1. Run a measured distance and back.
2. Do 5 Frog Jumps (#130) on the grass.
3. Throw a ball into a hoop or basket.
4. Do 10 Jumping Jacks (#126).
5. Crawl under an outdoor table.
6. Throw a ball as far as you can.
7. Kick a ball as far as you can.
   Repeat the entire sequence 3 times.

Alphabetical List of Games

List of Games Arranged by Specific Categories

Games Requiring a Large Space

87	Outdoor Playground	195	Traveling Tennis
120	Jump Rope, Both Feet Low	196	Tennis Dribbling
121	Jump Rope, Both Feet High	198	Moon Ball
122	Jump Rope, One Foot Only	199	Grounder
123	Jump Rope, Alternating Feet	200	Circle Kicking
125	Jump Rope, Scissor Jumps	206	Tire Running
140	Biking	208	Kangaroo Jumps
141	Hiking	214	Two-Ball Bounce
145	Leap with High Knees	215	Nondominant Hand/Nondominant Foot
154	Chicago Squat Walk		
155	Jack Travel	216	All-Out Dribble
156	Knee-Ups	217	Backward Basketball
157	Circle Cardio	218	Basketball Balance
159	Motion Combination	219	Blindfolded Basketball
160	Quadriceps Challenge	220	Two-Ball Toss
161	Box Step	221	Frisbee Toss
162	New York, New York	222	Swing and a Hit
163	Ski Prep	223	Interval Runs
164	Face of a Clock	224	High-Knees Running
165	Stale Fish	225	Take a Hike
166	Hot Dog	227	Power Jumps
167	Caboose	228	Jump-Ups
168	Slide Combination	229	Broad Jumps
169	Killer Legs	230	180-/360-Degree Turn
170	The Gym	231	Single-Leg Hops
172	Aerobics-Class Combination	232	Popcorn
190	Watch the Racquet	233	Forward Rolls/Somersaults
191	Soccer Stop	234	Backward Rolls
192	Drop Kicks	235	Cartwheels
193	Knee Bumps	236	Round-Offs
194	Tennis	237	Assisted Handstands

Games in Which Physical Contact Might Be Involved

Games Requiring an Exercise Mat

Games Requiring Props

Games Requiring Musical Accompaniment

CPSIA information can be obtained
at www.ICGtesting.com
Printed in the USA
JSHW031826280721
17348JS00003B/251